Stepping on the Stones

A New Experience in Recovery

Third Edition

Developed by: Joanna Johnson, MSW, MAC, CAC, CFAS, CFC

© *2010 by Joanna Johnson, MSW, MAC, CAC, CFAS, CFC. All Rights Reserved.*

No part of this book may be reproduced, stored in a retrieval system, or transmitted by any means without written permission of the author.

Original edition first published by Author House 7/16/2010
Second Edition published by Createspace 3/24/2014
Third Edition published by Createspace 1/7/2018

Personal Message

Dear Reader,

Everything that follows on these written pages represents the collective thinking of recovering addicts and alcoholics. The concept of the stepping stones is based on the knowledge and understanding that our entire group is in recovery. This manual represents what did and did not work throughout approximately one hundred years of combined recovery experience. We have all been in and out of many programs. This is as grass roots as it gets. We welcome you to the exploration and experience of moving forward in recovery.

Joanna Johnson, MSW, MAC, CAC, CFAS, CFC

About the Author

Joanna Johnson is currently the director of Avalon Treatment Centers, in Tallahassee and Crawfordville, Florida. She has been in the field of addiction for 25 years and a recovery addict for over 30 years. She has been the director of treatment centers, prison modality, tribal child welfare, tribal mental health, and is currently an expert in many judicial circuits. She was published for the first time in Canada in 1986 by the University of Calgary Press.

Disclaimer

This workbook is based on a traditional recovery program. This workbook is meant to be a self-help manual on your road to recovery. It does not, however, take the place of a professional therapist who is trained in addiction counseling. If you or a loved one needs counseling (which is a great tool on this journey) then I encourage you to explore the concept of individual or group counseling.

Acknowledgements

This manual and the accompanying materials have been created by former alcoholics and addicts. The team who diligently worked on this project did so with a passion for you, dear reader, because we know what it is like to be overtaken by this dreaded disease called addiction. Many of us have worked very hard to ensure that this manual works for all age groups, races, and religions. These are the influences on this exciting new tool in the struggle to recovery.

Kinanaskomitin, Manito.

I want to thank:

- NA and AA for saving my life.
- My children and grandchildren for tolerating my insanity.
- Frog Lake for igniting my spirit.
- My Heiss family and my Quinney family.
- My sisters Rachel and Lena.
- The late Alice and Lloyd Quinney for unconditional love.
- The late Theresa Gadwa (my first real mentor).
- Nikki Tang and Dana Hanson for your tolerance.
- Every person like my late husband Clyde, who struggled with this disease until the day he died, and those who are still struggling.

You are all so important and special. I am so grateful to have walked my path and am still trying to keep my balance, Teniki.

Author Note

Since the first publication of this book in 2010, my staff and I have learned and grown so much in the field of addiction. This republication is my way of sharing the new knowledge that my staff and I have acquired. Over the years we have come to rely on and trust in the assessment process. I feel this is the one of most important factors in your recovery. During an assessment, the treatment provider will work to learn not only what you need help with, but also who you are, and why drug and alcohol addiction became a destructive element in your life. Any conditions that can perpetuate drug and alcohol abuse such as mental illness, health problems, family history, abuse history, spiritual affiliations, etc. will be discovered and used to create a personalized treatment plan, which is the second most important factor in a successful treatment program.

As my manual will teach you, drug and alcohol addiction is a disease. There are multiple potential counterparts to the disease that are discussed during an assessment to determine the appropriate level of care. For example, mental health issues that may require medication, religious affiliations, genetic predispositions, etc. Considering these special factors during each case means that I can recommend precisely the level of care each client needs based on an all-inclusive understanding of their addiction. In conclusion, an assessment is an irreplaceable tool and the first step towards recovery.

My staff and I are a very tight team and have been so for at least 15 years. When 4 people work as such a tight unit it has allowed us to cover many different variates of addiction and bring that to this workbook. I feel it is also important to note, that my practice has never received a dime of finding from the government but have become a primer expert in the field of addiction but have achieved feats such as being named Professional of the Year for the Northwest Region as part of the Florida Drug and Alcohol Addiction Abuse Association's 2011 Award for Excellence.

Now finally let me explain why I have republished this book: Over the years we have noticed a lot of agencies do not offer or work with relapse prevention. This was a mistake even my practice made in the first publications of this book. This new publication is meant to rectify that error. The field of addiction is always a learning process and I want to grow with you. I have seen how relapse prevention helps clients with slips and relapse, as well as understanding the difference. As a team my practice has decided that this needs to be more prominent and therefore have transformed our final stone (Stone 7) in to just that, RELAPSE PREVENTION. I believe this is critical to helping clients remain clean and sober.

Over the years I feel that Stepping on the Stones has become an evidence based practice. This is based on the following:

1. Thousands of administered assessments;
2. Being an active part of the court systems for over 15 years;
3. Being an active part of legal teams working with complicated addiction cases;
4. Monitoring and recording the success of our client in relation to our material and other materials offered;
5. The fact that this publication has been used and praised by thousands and references are available through attorneys, judges, and private entities;
6. I use this publication and use it to teach inmates at a prison run by the Department of Corrections;
7. My practice is licensed and inspected with an 80% percent rating or above each year at both of my centers;
8. For many years we have had government officials come and sit in on our groups;
9. Prominent schools in our local area and beyond send their students to intern and sit in on our classes and programs; and
10. I was named Professional of the Year for the Northwest Region as part of the Florida Drug and Alcohol Addiction Abuse Association's 2011 Award for Excellence.

Index

1. Introduction……………………………………………………………… Page 6

2. Healthier Life Contract …………………………………………………. Page 10

3. The Importance of Treatment …………………………………………… Page 11

4. Drug/Alcohol Addiction Test …………………………………………… Page 13

5. Addiction ………………………………………………………………… Page 15

6. The First Stone ………………………………………………………….. Page 18

7. The Second Stone ……………………………………………………….. Page 37

8. The Third Stone …………………………………………………………. Page 74

9. The Fourth Stone ………………………………………………………… Page 9

10. The Fifth Stone …………………………………………………………. Page 124

11. The Sixth Stone ………………………………………………………… Page 201

12. The Seventh Stone ……………………………………………………… Page 212

Inventories – Pages 257-264

Introduction

Your First Image

For you to fully understand the impact of this manual you will first need to conjure a mental and visual image of a creek. The one I use is called 32. It is in High Falls New York and is a fast running, cold body of water with stones across that would allow you to get from one side to the other. The banks are steep, and I would have to squat down and hold on to the roots to get to the first stone. Some of the stones were always slippery and hard to stay on, as are some of our personal issues are difficult to face.

We will always slip into the water because our feet are not securely planted on the stone. We will slip from one issue and even fall, but if we remain clean and sober we can just dry off and start again. That creek is not going away. If we are going to get across we must do all the work. This disease is not going away so if you are going to begin and stay on this journey you will have to do all the work. You are in that position now. Squatting and holding on is just what we are doing when we are struggling with addiction.

Go into your garden or a field and pick up 7 stones. Bring them in and wash them, then with a marker paint numbers 1-7 on each stone. Stone 1 should always be in the brightest color. You will be able to move the stones around as you need to, and they will always help to visually take you to the areas of awareness you are working on at any given time.

As you begin to work this manual you will start to see a new pattern develop in your thinking and you will begin to relate increasingly with the concept of the stones. Be patient with yourself. This is a process. It is also an adventure to cross that creek. Recovery is always going to have its deep currents and will be deepening every day. Some stones will be slippery and some dry and easy to mount.

The workbook you hold will guide you out of the darkness and into the light. It is your confidential journey. Complete honesty and truthfulness, although difficult, are of the utmost importance. As you work through the questions, remember you are giving yourself a wonderful, life-changing gift - the gift of freedom from compulsive and obsessive patterns that always bring us back to drugs and alcohol, food, sex, work, gambling, or other ways of escaping.

I am a recovering addict with over 30 years clean and sober. I understand slippery stones and the immense struggle to keep your footing. My journey started at age 12 and it took 18 years of self-destruction until I found my stones. High Falls was where it all happened for me in 1968. The idea of the stones began to form in my mind while getting high and living the hippy lifestyle, before moving to Alberta, Canada. I appreciate and will always use the 12 steps but 30 years in that program brought me to understand why this program was needed and long overdue.

Like the twelve steps, at some point you may want to have someone of your choice to be a mentor, but this is the age of cyberspace, so you virtually can have many recovery mentors.

encourage you to seek and utilize your relationship with your Higher Power for the ability to let go of the things you don't need to carry (mental and spiritual baggage). I want you to do this, so you are free to become healthy. If you are holding this workbook to help someone in your life battle this disease, I encourage you to not give up hope.

For years the traditional self-help venue was 12 steps, AA, NA, and combinations of the above. This program just goes a little further and allows each of us to look deeper within ourselves without being formally involved with AA or NA. This manual, your favorite mirror, and a place you call your safe zone will take you to group immediately.

**If you really want to be happy then take
the risk and begin the journey.**

It begins with looking in a mirror and asking yourself who you are. Each time a negative response comes to mind ask repeatedly. The mirror will become your self-image and it will transform from an image you don't want to see, to the person you really want to see each day. Each stone will represent a calming factor while working the program.

At stressful times (which may be frequent during this process) it would be beneficial to partake in some sort of physical activity. *For example: going for a walk, using the treadmill, martial arts, yoga, dancing, etc. Anything you do that gets your heart rate up will help you deal with stress.*

Remember that addiction (compulsive obsessive behavior) is about everything and manifests itself in all levels of society. If you are reading this workbook for recovery and want to meet an addict, go look in the mirror - and introduce yourself. I know that reality of the awareness of this disease is something that you will have trouble accepting and developing an understanding of, but this is your first step.

Addiction is not what you had intended for your life, as none of us do. Being able to grasp the concept that you have the disease rather than just a behavior is hard to swallow and that's okay. Recovery comes slowly, daily, moment by moment. Just like my experience in the creek, it is important that you are patient with yourself as you begin your new journey.

The road will have hills, valleys, sometimes dead-ends, dark rivers, and small creeks. But no matter what, you will cross them all. Each one may be in a different way, but in the end, it will be you who will be the next adventure. Each new day presents an opportunity to begin again. Walk the stepping stones slowly like a brook. They will be slippery, but as you get surer footed your balance will come back. Enjoy the experience.

How to Use This Manual

As you begin this incredible journey here are a few suggestions we found helpful. First, questions asked of you in the workbook are essential for your recovery. Answering them with honesty is important. This will eventually give you a great insight into issues about your disease that have been hidden by the behaviors of addiction. The space provided for these questions are only the beginning.

Use a notebook for additional space. If you intend to use this manual over and over (as we hope you will) then please answer all questions in your notebook. In the back of the workbook you will find your inventory sheets. When an inventory is called for, pull out a sheet and complete it. I suggest you have the following tools:

- Seven stones all washed and labeled 1-7;
- Pencils (allows you to erase and re-write);
- Journal or notebook for additional writing;
- Special treats for yourself for rewarding the completion of a STONE;
- A Pocket Dictionary. This may be helpful for words in this manual if you are unsure of their definition;
- "Healthier Life" contract. Sign, date and hang this contract where you can view it often. A reminder of this commitment will aid you in tougher-than-normal days; and
- Take the Drug/Alcohol Addiction Test before and after completing this workbook

The Stones

The stones are about energy and are symbolic to the creek you are about to cross over. In other words, they help you to understand out of control compulsive obsessive behaviors and bringing you to a new level within yourself, which is the journey to recovery and self-worth. The stones you'll use to represent this journey should not be big and should fit in your hand.

If you want, use a marker, paint, crayon, or whatever you have and write a number on each stone. Each stone will be part of your image of walking the creek, and you will handle them a lot. As you are working a stepping stone, keep handling the stone. I choose to keep my stones in a circle, which is how I can most relate. My friends use straight lines and all kind of combinations. You will decide this for yourself. My first stone, by the way, is always with me as I always work and live within the teachings of the first stone.

How to Do an Inventory

An inventory is a visual picture of your life experiences divided into different phases of time as identified by age brackets. Under each topic that you identify, go to the right side of your inventory sheet, and find the age that you want to relate information positive and negative to. In the back of your manual are 10 inventory sheets. Please use these and if you need more, just copy them.

Once you have completed an inventory look at the page. It is then easy to see your patterns and your personal accomplishments and personal failures. This will be a writing map for your questions and then for your recovery. This first inventory is the hardest. The concept of personal inventories is a process you will continue throughout recovery and it becomes your key tool to knowing yourself. An inventory is self-disclosure. An inventory looks at an age span of your life and documents events and behaviors and feelings during that timeframe. It directs you toward a specific timeframe and associates the issues during that timeframe you will self-examine. We have given you an example inventory in the back; use it to see how to fill in the categories.

A sample and blank inventory pages are located at the back of the book, pages 257-264

Healthier Life Contract

I _____, commit myself to begin the wonderful journey of recovery.

I am committing to myself to:

- Be clean and sober one day at a time
- Be honest in all my writing
- Give myself the right to cry
- Treat myself with respect

I will begin my journey of recovery by understanding that I will have difficult and very hard days, accepting that having very hard days will be all right. Perfection is elusive and unobtainable and therefore my goal is to begin each day anew, knowing that recovery is a process, not instantaneous.

_____   _____
Signature   Date

The Importance of Treatment

"There is a crack in everything God has made"

What are the stepping stones and why do we need to understand them as a prerequisite to recovery? Why is it important to understand the disease concept? It is important, so we can learn to live with the disease of alcoholism and chemical dependency.

Addiction is more than a physical dependence on drugs. Psychological and social factors are often powerful stimuli for drug/alcohol relapse. Stress, especially sudden life stresses, cues in the environment (like visiting a neighborhood), social networks, and spending time with friends who continue to use drugs can create ongoing, nearly irresistible urges to use drugs/alcohol. Treatment helps you to escape cravings and learn to cope with life, without using drugs.

The Disease

What makes us addicts is the *disease* of addiction and not the actual drugs or alcohol. Alcohol and drugs are what we do. It is not about behavior. It is about compulsive and obsessive action and about the way we think. Addiction is a disease of the brain and relates directly to our thinking and the way we interpret and disseminate information. It is the same thinking pattern that makes us prone to obsession and compulsion in all areas of our lives. (Taken from the Narcotics Anonymous (NA) workbook)

Definition of Addiction: Being abnormally tolerant to and dependent on something that is psychologically or physically habit forming. The term addiction is used in many ways to describe an obsession or compulsion or excessive physical dependency. *Example: smoking, eating, computer, video games, and some TV. Doing anything out of balance is the key.*

Definition of Compulsive: The pattern of thinking that causes you to do things, not because you want to, but because you feel you must. Compulsive drug addiction is as above, but has the potential to harm oneself despite their desire to stop. This also applies to all other actions. *Example: eating past full, drinking until drunk and working too much.*

Definition of Obsessive: A persistent disturbing preoccupation with an often-unreasonable idea, feeling, or task. *Example: The typical person forms tasks to seek relief from obsessive anxiety. This is about intrusive thoughts which can interfere with a person's clarity of mind. This is about imbalance.*
Preoccupation is the key word. *Example: I want what I want when I want it. Another example would be seeing a pair of shoes and not getting the shoes off your mind until you go back to the store and buy them, regardless of having money for the shoes but having to have the shoes.*

Let's talk first about your history:

How long have you been getting high?

_____

_____

_____

_____

How long have you realized you have a problem with compulsive obsessiveness?

_____

_____

_____

_____

How has this affected your life?

_____

_____

_____

_____

Drug/Alcohol Addiction Test
Take the Quiz

Note: This test will only be scored correctly if you answer each one of the questions.

Please check one response for each item.

1. Have you used drugs other than those required for medical reasons? ☐ Yes ☐ No
2. Have you abused prescription drugs? ☐ Yes ☐ No
3. Do you abuse more than one drug at a time? ☐ Yes ☐ No
4. Can you get through the week without using drugs? ☐ Yes ☐ No
5. Are you always able to stop using drugs when you want to? ☐ Yes ☐ No
6. Have you had "blackouts" or "flashbacks" as a result of drug use? ☐ Yes ☐ No
7. Do you ever feel bad or guilty about your drug use? ☐ Yes ☐ No
8. Does your spouse (or parents) ever complain about your involvement with drugs? ☐ Yes ☐ No
9. Has drug abuse created problems between you and your spouse or your parents? ☐ Yes ☐ No
10. Have you lost friends because of your use of drugs? ☐ Yes ☐ No
11. Have you neglected your family because of your use of drugs? ☐ Yes ☐ No
12. Have you been in trouble at work because of your use of drugs? ☐ Yes ☐ No
13. Have you lost a job because of drug abuse? ☐ Yes ☐ No
14. Have you gotten into fights when under the influence of drugs? ☐ Yes ☐ No
15. Have you engaged in illegal activities to obtain drugs? ☐ Yes ☐ No
16. Have you been arrested for possession of illegal drugs? ☐ Yes ☐ No
17. Have you ever experienced withdrawal symptoms (felt sick) when you stopped taking drugs? ☐ Yes ☐ No
18. Have you had medical problems because of your drug use (e.g., memory loss, hepatitis, convulsions, bleeding, etc.)? ☐ Yes ☐ No
19. Have you gone to anyone for help for a drug problem? ☐ Yes ☐ No
20. Have you been involved in a treatment program especially related to drug use? ☐ Yes ☐ No

About Scoring this Drug Addiction Test Questionnaire

This quiz is scored by allocating 1 point to each 'yes' answer -- except for questions 4 and 5, where 1 point is allocated for each 'no' answer -- and totaling the responses.

In other words, please score one point for each if you answered the following:

       1) Yes   2) Yes   3) Yes   4) No   5) No   6-20) Yes

Drug Addiction Symptoms Test Score

1-5 = Low Level
6-10 = Moderate Level
11-15 = Substantial Level
16-20 = Severe Level

Anything above the substantial level indicates a serious problem. Even at moderate levels though you should get help - because inevitably before long you will be at the substantial level and above - and it becomes that much harder to beat your addiction.

Addiction

Addiction is a chronic disorder precipitated by a combination of genetic, biological, and social factors. Obsessive compulsive behavior characterizes it.

Stages of Addiction

Stage 1: Use - when a person uses drugs or alcohol either in a social environment or under a doctor's care. The user realizes quickly that a substance can change the reality of any situation. The more the user takes a drug or increases drinking the more they feel they are in control when it is really the drug that has the control

Stage 2: Misuse - when one self-medicates or exceeds the prescribed amount. This stage involves taking drugs over the prescribed amount or buying illegal drugs. Tolerance begins to be developed and the user may suffer from hangovers.

Stage 3: Abuse - continued use of alcohol or other drugs despite negative consequences. Begins with an increase in frequency of substance use, solitary use may occur as well as loss of control. Mood swings become more frequent as well as hiding use. Consequences appear in the form of deterioration of relationships, problems at work, etc. Denial grows.

Stage 4: Dependency/Addiction - compulsive and obsessive use of substance. At this stage an individual may use substances just to feel normal rather than to reach a euphoric feeling. Loss of control usually sets in such as; arrests, theft, prostitution, etc. The individual has paranoid feelings and isolates themselves from the world.

The Stages of Change

Stage 1: Pre-contemplation - users do not intend to change behavior and may not feel there is even a problem

Stage 2: Contemplation - users acknowledge a problem and want to make a change but are not sure of how or when to do it

Stage 3: Preparation - users make a commitment to change and begin to make a plan for treatment

Stage 4: Action - users begin to change their usual habits as well as environment

Stage 5: Maintenance - users work to continue sobriety and prevent relapse

Recovery

Recovery is the process in which an individual realizes that they have a problem with drugs or alcohol and begin to take necessary steps to overcome their dependency and work through all the underlining problems of obsessive, compulsive, and manipulative behaviors and habits.

When I think of addiction, what do I feel, and what comes to mind?

___

What other areas in your life, besides the use of alcohol or drugs, do you recognize as compulsive in nature and obsessive in actions?

___

How does your compulsive and obsessive thinking act out each day? Remember, alcohol and drugs are only one form of compulsive behavior. *For example: I went to lunch and next door was the mall. I did not need anything, but I told myself I had a few minutes, so I would just look. I walked out with $300.00 dollars' worth of clothing, none of which I needed, all of which I wanted. This happens a lot.*

___

Look at your life and look at all the categories which you would consider to be obsessive and compulsive. How have they affected your family, relationships, work, and education, mental physical and spiritual health? To better assist you with organizing your thoughts, see the sample inventory in the back of the manual.

GO TO: INVENTORY LOCATED ON PAGES 257-264

Now let's do a positive self-assessment. We all possess positive traits. Look at the areas of your life that you are good at. (*Statistically, people with the disease of addiction have more than average intelligence, creativity, and emotional intuitiveness.*) List your positive traits.

_____

_____

_____

_____

So why are we so hard on ourselves?

_____

_____

_____

_____

The First Stone

In this first stone we will learn to admit to being powerlessness over our compulsive obsessiveness (addiction). To admit means to grant entrance to a place in the mind and to confess to oneself or others that you have done something right or wrong. To tell on oneself or to disclose or reveal. *Example: to admit you have gained weight instead of buying bigger clothing or to admit to something you did not do so another person will like you.* We need to learn how to tell ourselves the truth, which means admitting to ourselves we may have a problem and embracing something new like beginning a journey of recovery.

What does this mean to you personally?

_____

_____

_____

_____

_____

To admit means to tell on ourselves and ask, "Why is that important?" If we are not willing to "tell" on ourselves and discuss and accept that we have a problem, then we can't go any further. These questions will aid you in determining if you have a problem.

Write down five things you have had to admit that were difficult. How did you feel after you admitted your actions? Why you did decide to tell on yourself, who did you tell, and were you 100 percent honest?

_____

_____

_____

_____

_____

Have you admitted to yourself that you have a problem with drugs or alcohol? Explain.

___

Types of Denial

Denial of Fact

In this type of denial, someone avoids a fact by lying. Lying can take the form of an outright falsehood, leaving out certain details to tailor a story (omission), or by falsely agreeing to something. Someone who is in denial of fact is typically using lies to avoid truths that they think may be painful to themselves or others or detrimental to their character and/or reputation.

Denial of Responsibility

This type of denial involves avoiding responsibility by blaming, minimizing, or justifying. Blaming is a direct statement shifting fault, and may overlap with denial of fact. Minimizing is an attempt to make the effects or results of an action seem less harmful than they may be. Justifying is when someone takes a choice and tries to make that choice look okay due to their idea of what is "right" in a situation. Someone using denial of responsibility is generally attempting to avoid potential harm or pain by moving the attention away from themselves.

Denial of Impact

Denial of impact involves a person avoiding the knowledge of, or understanding the harms his or her behavior has caused to self or others. Doing this enables that person to avoid feeling remorse or guilt and it can prevent him/her from developing empathy for others. Denial of impact reduces or eliminates a feeling of pain or harm from poor decisions.

Denial of Awareness

This type of denial is best discussed by looking at the idea of being dependent upon being in a different state of mind to function or learn. People using this type of denial will avoid pain and harm by stating they were in a different state of awareness (such as alcohol or drug intoxication or on occasion mentally ill). This type of denial often goes hand in hand with denial of responsibility.

Denial of Cycle

Many who use this type of denial will say things such as, "it was a onetime thing" or "it won't happen again". Denial of cycle is where a person avoids looking at their decisions leading up to an event or does not consider the fact they have formed a pattern of decision making and repeat harmful behavior. They avoid pain and harm by using this type of denial and it is more of the effort needed to change the focus from a singular event to looking at past events. It can also be a way to blame or justify behavior.

Denial of Denial

This can be confusing for many people to identify with in themselves, but is a major barrier to changing harmful behaviors. Denial of denial involves thoughts, actions, and behaviors, which encourage one's confidence that nothing needs to be changed in their personal behavior. This type of denial goes hand in hand with all the other forms of denial, but involves more self-delusion.

Now use all the above definitions of denial in a self-inventory starting with your youth and ending in the present whether it is adolescent years, adult years, or senior years. Name the times you made up an excuse so that you could do what you intended to do from the beginning. *Example: Starting a fight with a spouse so that you could use the stress of the argument as a reason to use drugs or drink. "You made me" or "Because of you" I did this or that.*

GO TO: INVENTORY LOCATED ON PAGES 257-264

Re-live two incidents in which you told yourself a falsehood so that you could continue your obsessive behavior. This could include any compulsive behavior such as: eating, shopping, sex, working, drinking, drugging.

_____

_____

_____

_____

_____

_____

_____

I had a bad day at work so on my way home, I bought a pack of candy bars and ate them on my commute home. I told myself I deserved it. Although, I later felt depressed because I needed to lose 50 pounds.

A drug is a drug. Comparing addictions or drugs is about as ridiculous as it sounds. If I want to go to New York and I live in Florida, I may choose to take a plane. If you want to go to New York, you may choose to take a bus. We both will arrive at our chosen destination. It's not about how fast we get there; it is about the result. If you choose alcohol and I choose drugs, we both arrive at the end of a destructive path *(i.e., I'm not like them I just smoke weed, I never do cocaine).*

Do I compare my compulsive obsessiveness (addiction) to others' so I can justify myself and my current reality? Why do I compare?

_____

_____

_____

_____

_____

Do I use a "created value system" so I can justify my own addiction? *(Example: functional drunk, pills prescribed by a doctor, chronic pain)*

_____

_____

_____

_____

Justify means to demonstrate or prove to be right or valid, to clear myself of any blame and then be absolved of any guilt or penalty. *Example: "You made me angry, so I went out and got drunk. If you would do as I say I would not have to drink."*

Give personal examples of the things you have justified and then gave yourself the right to take no blame. *Example: blaming a sibling so you would not be caught for taking a cookie as a child, buying ice cream when on a diet and saying it was not for you but for company just to have in the house.*

Give four examples:

_____

_____

_____

_____

_____

_____

Enabling

To understand enabling just look at the wife who knows her husband had a drinking problem but continues to buy alcohol for him or bring it into their home. She does this thing by telling herself that he needs her and finds herself cleaning up the mess that occurs in the wake of their impaired judgment. So, what is the definition of enabling? It is about an intention to help but making the problem worse. The practical effect is that the person does not have to take any responsibility or blame and is shielded from awareness of the harm that they cause.

Who in your life enables you?

_____

_____

_____

_____

Why do they enable you to keep on keeping on?

_____

_____

_____

_____

What would change if they did not enable your issues?

___

Do you see yourself as an enabler?

___

Now it's time for you to do some research. Look up the definitions of the following words and write them in this workbook. After each definition explain how each one is part of your personality and how it has evolved positively and negatively.

RESPECT:

___

SELF:

___

WORTH:

_____

_____

_____

VALID:

_____

_____

_____

Now let's inventory and see the history of the above.

GO TO: INVENTORY LOCATED ON PAGES 257-264

GOOD WORK! Time for a break! Leave this alone for one hour. Listen to some music. Reflect on your hard work and treat yourselves well. You deserve this, you always have. Don't forget to keep handling your stone while working every inventory (this is very important).

NOW, Let's move forward!

Powerlessness

Powerlessness is about a driving force in our lives that is beyond our control. The quality of lacking strength or power, it is the sensation of being out of control without any apparent solution or plans to regain control. Powerlessness is also about the lack of capability to affect the reality of life that you cannot do anything about. *Example, the weather, if you get a certain job, if you're in an accident, or if you are going to get the flu.* To make this work for you, you need to first accept that you are powerless. *Example: If you did not get the job, rather than feeling sorry for yourself, what could you have done differently?*

What are the negative aspects of not accepting personal powerlessness?

_____

_____

_____

_____

What is the result of this attitude? How is accepting powerlessness a control issue?

___

___

___

___

Recognizing that you cannot change something gives you the ability to plan, to accept or reject, to reach out and ask for help, or just to try again. Now you can accept help because being powerless allows you to put aside your pride and ego and accept information, communication, and suggestions.

Accepting that you are powerless gives you self-esteem (which is another word for self-power). Take an honest look at how much control you have over problems with situations, people, places, and things. This will bring the reality of each moment, issue, or circumstance to you right then.

Now look at your first stone. Is it slippery or dry? Do you feel strong, secure, and confident enough to go on? Why or why not?

___

___

___

___

We are powerless when the forces that drive us seem to always take control. Some people see this as a weakness. Do you? Why or Why not?

___

___

___

___

There are a lot of things in my life I am powerless over, like other people and how they live their lives. Write some examples that really confuse you or are difficult for you to understand. Why do they do what they do? How you can accept what they do?

_____

_____

_____

_____

List some personal experiences with things that we are powerless over?

_____

_____

_____

_____

List some things in our lives we have tried to control and could not (Do not use alcohol or drugs).

_____

_____

_____

_____

Have you tried to stop a compulsive behavior perhaps with some success for a while but then it does not work? What is this about? Give examples.

_____

_____

_____

_____

What am I powerless over?

_____

_____

_____

_____

If I admit I was powerless, am I now in better shape mentally, and how does this affect me emotionally, spiritually, physically, mentally?

_____

_____

_____

_____

Have I ever tried to stop using or eating or working or acting out on my obsessiveness? Describe and discuss.

_____

_____

_____

_____

If I understand powerlessness and I disclose in my journal my secrets and concerns that make my thinking unmanageable how will my life change?

_____

_____

_____

_____

Now that I understand how powerlessness affects my life, how will I handle situations that create immediate panic responses?

_____

_____

_____

_____

Take a break, breathe, have a treat, and come back to the manual again when you are ready.

If you have succeeded to this point and you have not fully admitted powerlessness, or are in denial over the first self-disclosures in this manual, it's okay to slip off this stone. Grasp the stone in your hand, it may help you relax. Go back to the creek in your mind, start to walk the stones again. There are no repercussions in this manual for starting over or going back to something you may have to think about more. If you feel you need to address any of the previous categories, GO BACK!

Unmanageability

My definition of unmanageability is two-fold. Firstly, outward unmanageability is what is obvious to me and others. While inward unmanageability is the big secrets I keep and never talk about. These are the thoughts that are difficult to use or handle because of the weight of the problem. This could be because it's hard to control or difficult to solve, so I self-impose a solution. *Examples of self-imposed solutions: overeating, sex, drugs, work, and gambling. If I am in a forest and I am surrounded by tall trees, it is hard to find my way out, so I stay lost.* Powerlessness and unmanageability go hand in hand to keep you in a state of panic.

How will I stop treating personal and social challenges as an insult? How will I begin to accept criticisms as a constructive and not a destructive part of recovery?

_____

_____

_____

_____

What is my plan for living with the reality that my life becomes unmanageable when I do not accept that I am powerless over a lot of things; especially chemical dependency and substance abuse?

_____

_____

_____

_____

_____

_____

_____

_____

_____

CONGRATULATIONS! GREAT WORK!

My very favorite point of the first stone is the part that separates your ability to move on to Stone Two. The part working and holding the stone that is. It has taken you back to who you are as a person before the labels, the disappointments, the self-destruction, before spinning out of control. It has slowed you down. You will need to learn to live with the first experience of the first stone every day many times a day. This might be the stone you keep in your pocket, so you can feel it when you need to pull out your daily tools. This is a great time to take a break. My suggestion would be ice cream, but whatever you like is fine.

Spiritual Principles

What do we mean about spiritual? This is not a religious experience I am talking about. I am talking about a higher understanding of mental concepts, also, moral feelings such as personal values and principles. Values are ideals excepted by you as an individual or culture.

Types of values are:

- **Personal values** are the things you accept based on your past experiences and current life situations. An example of this would-be co-dependency.
- **Ethical Values** are the standards you live by and are not conditional.
- **Moral Principles** are about right and wrong. Here is where we talk about your judgment and how you decide to do what you do.
- **Social Values** are what you accept in your everyday life. Basically, what you expect of yourself and other people.
- **Judgmental Values** are the way you see things and how you see and accept information and communication.
- **Cultural Values** are your ethnic identity. *Example: If you are Native American your pow-wows and sun dances (rituals) or if you are Irish, St. Patrick's Day is a celebration special to your heritage.*

This is a good place to inventory your own personal understanding of values. What they mean to you now and have meant in the past. Please include the ones listed and any that you would like to add. *Example: work, family, money, relationships.*

GO TO: INVENTORY LOCATED ON PAGES 257-264

Now let's look at **Moral Myths:** This is all about truth. It's about full disclosure. It's about realizing that no one can be almost pregnant; you either are or are not. This is where you need to look honestly inside and pick apart your personal values.

Do you still tell half-truths? Give examples.

Do you still tell people what they want to hear because it is safer, and you still care about being liked? Give examples.

Are you willing to hear other people's opinions and realize you might need to do that even if you don't want to? Give examples.

Are you open minded and able to accept new concepts and new directions? Even if it means leaving an old family tradition such as your own background or belief system and are ready to address that?

Now it's time to inventory family myths and false beliefs that have been with you all your life.

GO TO: INVENTORY LOCATED ON PAGES 257-264

What about my ego and my family system? Are you able to open your mind? How about your family, are they able to change their perspective or are they stubborn/set in their way? Give examples.

_____

_____

_____

_____

What and how is it important for you to become humbler? How are you going to embrace humility and how hard will this be?

_____

_____

_____

_____

What am I still not able to accept and what am I still unable to share?

_____

_____

_____

_____

Am I able to accept all factors of my disease honestly?

___

What is it about recovery that I do not feel applies to me or I just do not understand?

___

What are some of my trust issues?

___

What are some of my relationship problems that I need to be honest about?

___

What are some of the problems with friends I need to get honest about?

What is it about me I don't believe other people understand?

Why do I still care what other people think?

Have I really been honest with the whole issue of being powerless?

Are there still issues I am in denial about and not ready to address? If so, what are they?

_____

_____

_____

_____

_____

Am I ready for Stone Two and have I honestly addressed all the questions in Stone One? Can I now move on, or do I have to go back to the visual edge of the creek, regain my balance, and rediscover the first stone?

What are my thoughts of what I have discovered so far?

_____

_____

_____

_____

_____

_____

_____

_____

_____

_____

Contract with Self to Move on to the Second Stone

In signing this contract, with myself I am stating that I believe that I am ready to move on. I understand and am being honest with all the questions. I feel that I am done with work on the first stone.

_____   _____
Signature   Date

The Second Stone

Stone Two is all about empowerment and learning how to develop a personal relationship with your spiritual beliefs and/or rebirth of your faith so that you can restore a balance and sanity into your life. What is balance? It is when all parts are equal, for example, when you can get angry without rage, or hungry without pigging out, tired and go to sleep, and hurt without escaping. It is when love is not co-dependency and when relationships are partnerships.

Here is my view on this:

I know that my being here today was no accident, and that somehow a higher power or in my concept, the creator, had a plan for me. I know that all the dangerous, dysfunctional, dishonest, and deceitful, dark places I have been, were all a part of where I am now. I know that I have had a power greater than myself with me every step of the way.

First, despite all the drugs I have done, the abuse I survived, the abuser I became as a child, the lying, the fake identities, and all the dangerous situations I have put myself in - I am here writing this manual. I have always understood that insanity is where I thought I was until I learned to understand more about the disease of addiction and how this disease affected everything in my world, every day, all the time. And still does every day. A power greater than myself started with just a white chair, music, walks, mountains, and so many small and indefinable things, all the things that gave me a glimpse of hope. Maybe I could do this. This was the beginning of the process of recovery and the beginning of the process of understanding this insane lifestyle could stop.

Think of a moving train, to get off the train, the train must come to a total stop. Jumping off a moving train endangers you and destroys you physically, mentally, and spiritually. If the jump does not kill or wound you, the sudden stop will. Addiction is the same. If just getting clean is enough, then why do we still have so much collateral damage? **We resist the second stone because we confuse spirituality and higher power with religious beliefs.** The 12 steps do not require anyone to be religious. The stepping stone concept is about you and your creation of your own needs and beliefs.

Awareness can start with anything. A chair that gives you a place to think and breathe or music that takes you to a place where you can think are powerful if they bring enlightenment. Remember, it does not matter how long or how insane, with a belief in the power of understanding and spiritual principles you will restore yourself to the sanity you seek.

Something fabulous happened to me when I realized for the first time I was not crazy. I realized I was out of control, my thinking and perspectives were out of proportion, and all my priorities were messed up. When I slowed down and allowed myself to release the need of control, believed things would get better, followed the suggestions of others who were where I was before me, I could find a way back. When I look back it was change and the idea of being honest that terrified me.

Even if I didn't know the difference between my needs and wants at the time, I did believe in the hope that something was beginning to change. It all starts with respect. The respect to have self-esteem and self-worth. We all need to reconnect with our own personal quality and ability to live life on its own terms. There is no limit to the ability of our self-respect. This will restore our lives back into to balance.

In our program a higher power represents anything that each of you believe is adequate, such as, nature, freedom from oppression, friendships, God, science, Buddha, or any religious interpretation. A higher power must be greater than yourself. It only needs to be loving and nurturing, and always must offer a feeling of goodness and something you can believe in. When you first try to define your higher power, you may have to go back and look at all the things that you have experienced and cannot explain.

Examples: Birth of a child, overcoming a traumatic experience, getting your first job, your first kiss, or meeting your first true love.

Name your own and explain how it made you feel.

_____

_____

_____

_____

Where do you find peace of mind? *Examples: mountains, beaches, fields, lakes, sunny days, church, my mother's kitchen.*

_____

_____

_____

Now look at the things that have come in the way of the above questions.

_____

_____

_____

_____

Insanity

<u>Insanity</u> is doing the same things and expecting different results.

How has insanity never worked before and why did you think it would work this time?

_____

_____

_____

_____

It's time to look back at your needs and wants and separate them. *Example: I never needed to get high. I wanted to get high.*

Name them here:

_____

_____

_____

_____

Do you have balance in your life now when you look at everything overall?

_____

_____

_____

_____

What are the areas of your life that you need to bring balance back into, not including alcohol or drugs?

_____

_____

Where are your strong areas of self-growth and awareness?

_____

_____

_____

_____

Let's talk about life experiences, a part of our growth that we overlook. We see the positive experiences as very limited and the negative experiences as overwhelming, and don't realize they both have had an equal part of bringing us to this wonderful place.

Inventory time! Take a breath, get an apple, and grab the stone. Here we go!

GO TO: INVENTORY LOCATED ON PAGES 257-264

When did your dysfunctional lifestyle start feeling normal and what is this about?

_____

_____

_____

_____

If one does something long enough and becomes comfortable with the feeling and the emotions of its pattern it becomes normal to them. What were some of your behaviors and emotions that became normal?

_____

_____

_____

_____

How do you handle change in patterns now?

_____

_____

_____

_____

Let's look at your patterns. What situations have you created as part of your unstable life style in:

Work? _____

_____

_____

Family? _____

_____

_____

Economics? _____

_____

_____

Home? _____

_____

_____

Relationships? _____

_____

_____

Others? _____

The following information is taken straight from the NA 12 step workbook:

Insanity is a loss of our perspective and sense of proportion. So, we look at our problems as bigger, worse, more dangerous, and less fixable than anyone else. We compare addictions, we misread information. Therefore, we are unable to consider others. We do not care about other people's feelings, needs, and boundaries. We always see only ours. We are self-centered, and we are always out of balance. We create drama all the time.

Now let's try a new exercise in creating. Write a small commercial about your life and see what the point would be. End it with a positive message, even if the script is dark and hard to accept.

What is the drama of my life? Describe your own soap opera.

If you're the star in this drama describe your role and the character you play.

How do you interpret information? Describe your patterns.

_____

_____

_____

_____

What are you like when you feel people are not giving you the respect you deserve?

_____

_____

_____

_____

Part of the insanity the hurts that are part of your past.
Why have you chosen to keep reinventing them and their negative consequences?

_____

_____

_____

_____

Belief Systems

<u>Belief system:</u> A belief system is the basis on what and how you believe something. *Example: Religious belief is based on Bible interpretation. Scientific belief is based on observation and reason.*

Myths are personal beliefs, true or untrue, that we grow up with that form our judgment, opinions, observations, and way of life. *Example: Negative Myths - Men don't cry, women are more sensitive, secrets are always kept in families.* Negative belief systems are the base for prejudice, illegal activities, etc. *Positive myths - if you work hard you will always succeed.*

Is part of your insanity your belief system? Explain.

_____

_____

_____

_____

Is your belief system other people's interpretation of facts? (i.e., parent's racism, family patterns of drinking, neglected raising children, the need to get married if a partner becomes pregnant, religious doctrines, dispensary rules of the family) Describe them.

_____

_____

_____

_____

How do you define your beliefs and make them work for you as a new open-minded, understanding, and recovering person?

_____

_____

_____

_____

Many of us found that our understanding of insanity goes further than just every day patterns. We seem to be the black and blue generation. We make the same bad decisions over and over. For example, we keep falling back into bad company even when we try to do it right. We then just say "screw it" and don't care about the consequences. We feel that our obsessive behavior will overall work out.

Describe two incidents in which you made the same bad decision, more than once.

_____

_____

_____

_____

What was the result?

_____

_____

_____

_____

Is there any other information in which you think you need to write about on insanity?

_____

_____

_____

_____

_____

_____

_____

_____

_____

"Coming to Believe"

What is "Coming to Believe?" It's the wakeup call that says my way is not working so I need to try something else, and I am ready to embrace change. That's what it was for me; just being tired of the same old games, same results, same escapes, same payback, same day, and never understanding "just for today".

I needed to look and overcome what was holding me in the insanity, which was my normal life. I needed to look at the fears I had of coming to believe and see what they were.

What keeps you from coming to believe there is a better way? Answer this question using the family myths you have been brought up with.

_____
_____
_____
_____

Are you afraid of change? Why?

_____
_____
_____
_____

What does coming to believe mean to you personally?

_____
_____
_____
_____

Do you understand that this is a process and not an overnight miracle? Explain.

_____

_____

_____

_____

Do you have the patience and understanding of this program, so far, to be able to wait, learn, begin the process, and allow the program to help with this transition?

_____

_____

_____

_____

What do you believe that you cannot support with evidence or personal knowledge?

_____

_____

_____

_____

Have you ever experienced an event that was amazing and should have never happened?

_____

_____

_____

_____

Have you ever walked away from what should have or could have been life strengthening?

_____
_____
_____
_____

Have you ever allowed things to change your mind through knowledge, experience, or observation?

_____
_____
_____
_____

Are you coming to believe in yourself more every day? Explain, give examples.

_____
_____
_____
_____

Is there anything about this topic you want to write about?

_____
_____
_____
_____

A Second Look at a High Power

Each person has a story that is the base of their life experience. It is where you learn your behaviors, change myths, follow direction, experiment with life and death, and grow. These are the experiences that develop into what kind of power greater than ourselves that we believe in.

During my heavy drug years, I believed that the only power greater than me was negative and everything I did reflected that. Therefore, I could just keep blaming others and keep getting high. I became a skilled liar, thief, and manipulator. All of this I blamed on my karma and my destiny. Never understanding that my real destiny was being molded by this and my higher power was keeping me alive. When the change finally happened, I was able to move on and achieve what I have, which is a recovery period of more than 30 years, wonderful children, great grandchildren, and recovering people who come through my life, some with minimal success and some with fantastic achievements.

It is not about having a religious awakening, it's about realizing that I don't have all the answers, and sometimes I don't ask the right questions. I needed to sit back, stop being defensive, and stay clean that day. It's was amazing what was revealed to me when the time was right. I do not control anything as great as all the negative power and positive power is mind blowing.

I have seen the wonders of the rain forest of South America, Peru, and Ecuador, more than once. I have lived in the wonderful Canadian Rockies, which I have considered my home for over 20 years and have always been impressed by the Northern Lights. I have heard every story including all the first nations' tales. I have survived childhood sexual abuse. I have survived abusing my brother. I have survived being raped by a doctor while my mother waited in the lobby.

This was all made possible by just turning it over and realizing it was too big for me to deal with. It took work to trust. I knew it would be difficult but took giving responsibility from me to my high power to help me regain control. I never had to understand why the river was so beautiful I just had to enjoy it. I never had to understand the lights; I just had to watch them dance and enjoy both the negative and positive factors. I learned from them how wonderful and easy it made things.

What do you have a problem accepting?

_____

_____

_____

_____

What do you still not want to accept from the following?

Childhood? _____

_____

_____

Teen Years? _____

_____

_____

Married or Adult Years? _____

_____

_____

If you gave up the worry, how would things change for you?

_____

_____

_____

By holding on to the guilt have you stopped the healing?

_____

_____

_____

If you turned over what is bothering you, what do you think you could expect?

If you examine your expectations and keep them simple what can you expect?

Name five areas in your life in which you need sanity now.

Are you ready to turn your life around? Why or Why not?

_____

_____

_____

_____

Let's go even further into the question of a power greater than yourself and the restoring of sanity to your life. Let me set up a scenario about this wonderful oak table I found at a second-hand store. It was clearly abused, layers of paint weathered, and left in an outdoor shed. At the time, I was living with a man who was once a logger. I realized how wonderful the wood under all the damage was and that this table was just like me. To restore it to its original beauty steps would have to be taken, day by day, one day at a time to restore it to the original wood.

My restoration was restoring myself to the sanity I deserved and needed to be healthy, as well as staying a recovering addict. Each day I worked on this table. I stripped the paint and I sanded the wood and did it repeatedly until I was at the base wood. It was so lovely, but I knew I could not just leave it. It was so vulnerable to the elements in its natural form. I had to protect it by using natural oil, so it would stay beautiful if its recovery was kept up with. Now it was my turn to the deal with all the pain, distortions, layers of neglect, drugs, lack of responsibility, and damage I caused to all the people who loved me and depended on me. I was ready to be restored, which was the beginning of my road to recovery. Giving back, which is what I do, helps me remain on my journey.

What are the things you consider your sanity?

_____

_____

_____

_____

_____

_____

_____

What is your restoration plan?

How and why it will work?

_____

_____

_____

_____

What are the areas in which you still need a lot of work? Have you begun the stripping down of the layers?

_____

_____

_____

_____

What area(s) of your life do you feel are not ready to begin the process of restoration?

_____

_____

_____

_____

Expectations

<u>An expectation</u> is looking forward to an event that is about to happen. Expectations need to be measurable based on the event. If one expects more than they are ready for or if the expectation is too high then a feeling of failure, guilt, or shame can be a negative result.

By keeping your expectations measurable to what you are ready for and what you need in the balance of your life, you never set yourself up for disappointment. What if you have unrealistic expectations of restoring yourself to a whole person you need or want to be?

We set up barriers from the beginning, too high and too dense. For example, we will not get angry, we will not have problems that we obsess over, and we will now have balance in our lives. If we address all their expectations, we will eliminate all turmoil. STOP! You are distorting sanity and fantasy!

Sanity means having realistic expectations. For examples, understanding that when you get angry you do not have to turn to substances. You can let go of things that are too big for you to handle, you can slow down and breath. Look, listen, and learn.

Does this make sense to you? What are your thoughts?

_____
_____
_____
_____

Can you separate expectations, so you are not disappointed?

_____
_____
_____
_____

What are some expectations you need to rethink and scale down?

_____
_____
_____
_____

What areas do you need to challenge yourself more?

_____
_____
_____

What area(s) of your life have you been afraid to relook at? Are you ready to write about and work through these fears with your sponsor or fellow recovering friend?

My favorite part of the second stone is spiritual principles. It is where the truth is exposed, and procrastination stops. Here is where each of us focuses on open-mindedness, faith, trust, and humility. Open-minded people listen, learn, and ask for help. We need to forget about what we have learned from negative influences and focus on our own interpretation. For many of us this is new territory.

<u>Faith</u> is a very personal and self-gratifying part of this stone. Faith is only defined through your own experiences. Simply put faith is to believe in something.

<u>Trust</u> is a major issue for addicts. It means to have confidence or faith in.

<u>Humility</u> is the removal of and/or put down of our egos.

What about being open-minded? Where do you have to begin? What have you carried that is your interpretation of what you have learned over the years? Start with: Have you noticed addiction has no favorites? It will accept anyone, anytime, anywhere, and run you to the ground. You can always expect the same: jails, institutions, or death.
What are some of your spiritual principles pertaining to the following categories?

Environmental: _____

_____

_____

Relationships: _____

_____

_____

Gender specific roles: _____

_____

_____

Children of addict's: _____

_____

_____

Family: _____

_____

_____

Financial: _____

_____

_____

Trying new things: _____

_____

_____

Racial equality: _____

_____

_____

Sexual equality: _____

_____

_____

Word: _____

_____

_____

Culture: _____

_____

_____

How you have changed from being closed minded to being open-minded? Explain.

_____

_____

_____

_____

Do you question your faith? How?

_____

_____

_____

_____

Do you feel comfortable with seeking a more personal relationship with your higher power (of your understanding)?

_____

_____

_____

_____

Do you want to explore the religious denomination you were raised in? If not, what are some of the other possibilities that you might want to explore?

_____

_____

_____

_____

Make a list of the questions you have about faith and try to find the answers as you find an understanding of your higher power.

_____

_____

_____

_____

_____

_____

_____

Do you have a strong faith? Explain.

_____

_____

_____

How and why your faith has grown?

_____

_____

_____

Do you have faith in your recovery?

___

___

___

___

Now we need to look at some important life skills that are pertinent to your recovery:

Problem Solving

When we are faced with a situation that requires a resolution how do you figure it out? Do you quickly come to a decision? Do you review all the facts and how do you do that? Are you influenced by how others see a problem? Do you weigh options? Are you open to suggestions?

___

___

___

___

After all the above are you willing to compromise if that is what is apparent? Why or why not.

___

___

___

___

Decision Making

The following information is copied straight from "Anger Management for Substance Abuse and Mental Health Clients Participant Workbook." (ELLIS) and located at: **http://kap.samhsa.gov/products/manuals/pdfs/anger2.pdf**

    I.   The A-B-C-D Model

The A-B-C-D Model is consistent with the way some people conceptualize anger management treatment. In this model, *"A" stands for an activating event*. The activating event is the "event" or red-flag event. *"B" represents our beliefs* about the activating event. It is not the events themselves that produce feelings such as anger; it is our interpretations and beliefs about the events. *"C" stands for the emotional consequences*. These are the feelings experienced because of interpretations and beliefs concerning the event. *"D" stands for dispute*.

This part of the model involves identifying any irrational beliefs and disputing them with more rational or realistic ways of looking at the activating event. The idea is to replace self-statements that lead to, or escalate anger with ideas that allow you to have a more realistic and accurate interpretation of the event.

List some of your irrational beliefs.

_____

_____

_____

_____

How might you dispute these beliefs?

_____

_____

_____

_____

A-B-C-D Model

A = Activating Situation or Event

List an activating situation or event as explained above.

_____

_____

B = Belief System

What you tell yourself about the event (your self-talk)? Your beliefs and expectations of others?

_____

_____

C = Consequence

How you feel about the event based on your self-talk?

_____

_____

D = Dispute

Examine your beliefs and expectations. Are they unrealistic or irrational?

_____

_____

*Based on the work of Albert Ellis, 1979, and Albert Ellis and R.A. Harper, 1975.

Thought stopping

A second approach to controlling our anger is called "thought stopping." Thought stopping is an alternative to the A-B-C-D Model. In this approach, you simply tell yourself, through a series of self-commands, to *stop* thinking the thoughts that are making you angry. For example, you might tell yourself, "I need to stop thinking these thoughts. I will only get into trouble if I keep thinking this way," or "Don't buy into this situation," or "Don't go there."

In other words, instead of trying to dispute your thoughts and beliefs as outlined in the A-B-C-D Model above, the goal is to stop your current pattern of angry thoughts before they lead to an escalation of anger and a loss of control.

What are some other examples of thought-stopping statements you can use when you become angry?

_____

_____

_____

_____

Give three examples from a situation you have had where you reworked the problem with this formula.

_____

_____

_____

_____

Trust is a serious problem for most of us in recovery. The walls we have created must come down and we are afraid at the beginning to do so. We know how many people we have disappointed and how regaining their trust is going to take time, but the real problem is regaining trust in ourselves which must come first and remain first.

You cannot get clean for anyone else. Having everyone else's trust would be nice. However, unless you develop trust in your judgment calls and ability to make decisions based on real values you will never develop your ability to trust that if you make a mistake, it's ok. You do not have to use over it and most importantly, if you are clean today you can trust your recovery will grow stronger and stronger. Remember you must be willing to take a chance.

Addiction is not about risk; it is about predictability. We do the same things all the time and get the same results most of the time, until we either get clean, go to jail, or die. We spend money the same way, get the money the same way, lie to the same people, and manipulate for the same reasons. We never leave our dysfunctional comfort zone, which has become as normal as everyone else's lives.

Now we must take a risk. What are the risks that you're ready to take?

_____

_____

_____

_____

_____

_____

_____

_____

_____

_____

_____

_____

_____

_____

_____

_____

_____

_____

What are the changes that you can expect at first?

_____

_____

_____

_____

What are the changes that you can expect at first from your family?

_____

_____

_____

_____

What changes has recovery brought to your life to date?

_____

_____

_____

_____

What changes still need to take place?

_____

_____

_____

_____

Where do you need work as far as being open minded?

_____

_____

_____

_____

What are healthy risks for you?

_____

_____

_____

_____

What are unhealthy risks for you at this point of recovery?

_____

_____

_____

_____

Can you trust yourself to be around old friends?

_____

_____

_____

_____

Can you trust yourself to go to old places you visited in the past?

_____

_____

_____

_____

What signs do you have to trust your own instincts?

_____

_____

_____

_____

Humility

Understanding humility was hard for me as my ego always got in the way. I still wanted to be in control, and a small piece of me still thought that if I gave up all control, I was just a weak person. All this brought me back to Stone One and that's just where I need you to go if you feel the same way.

Now let's look at ego:

Ego is the overtones of one's self importance. This is the part of the mind that is most conscious, meditates, and takes in one's surroundings.

Where does your ego interfere with recovery?

_____

_____

_____

_____

_____

Do you need a strong ego, or do you need a balanced ego? Explain the difference.

___

Ego is "me me me". How do you relate to this?

___

Identify a time when your ego got in the way of a decision.

___

What is the state of your ego now?

___

Ego can also be referred to as pride. A lot of times we are too prideful to admit that we have a problem. The struggle with humility is putting your ego aside and listening and learning from the ones who have some established time in recovery, not necessarily those who have been sober a long time.

Are you able to stop and listen?

How hard is it for you to not always be right?

Do you ask your higher power for guidance?

Are you able to reach out for help from people you would have never asked help from before?

Have you sat down and honestly talked with your partner about your personal expectations?

_____

_____

_____

_____

If you have done all these questions, feel comfortable in your answers, and do not need more work in the first two stones, you're now ready for Stone Three. **GREAT WORK!** This took me months.

Honestly, I had to repeat these questions over and over for weeks at a time until I felt comfortable with this. Remember to feel the stone. Now it is time for a test of your honesty and personal humility. Are you ready to move on or should you be getting a new pad and pens?

The Third Stone

Wow! You are almost halfway across the creek! So now we are ready to review your decision-making skills.

The thing that gave me the most trouble with this stone was not the spiritual part, but making a major decision, because in the past all my decisions were a disaster. I was afraid that it was going to happen again as per my record of accomplishments.

For over twenty years, my addiction made all my decisions and I just followed the obsessive and compulsive road. I could not remember the last time I made a decision that was not compulsive. I did not know if I knew how to decide, and if I did; what if it was a wrong decision? What then?

The thought of being asked to make a critical decision and trusting my decision was a new concept that confused and scared me. I had stayed clean, answered questions, and went to group, but this was a serious matter. I realized that this decision was too big for me to make in one sitting. It was going to have to be part of the process. If I had understood no one expected me to be doing this all at once or quickly, I probably could have begun to absorb this. However, it was going to be as slow as it needed to be for me to understand recovery and that addiction is a disease.

My sponsor explained that all I was doing by making this decision was allowing myself to be taken care of and having some of the burden lifted from me. Slowly I came to understand this. My sponsor also explained to me that I needed to trust the process and have faith in myself. The Third Stone is a testimonial and personal test and with that explanation I stopped worrying about being forced to pick a religion or being forced to do anything I was not ready for.

I was still able to walk my journey at my pace. This was just going to lift some of the burden. I began to understand the key phrase here was 'of my understanding.' I was going to be the builder and I needed to take all the time I needed on this journey.

Making a Decision

I said earlier decision-making was difficult for me. I wanted someone else to do it, as did my addiction for twenty years. If someone else made the decision and it did not work I could just blame them and I did not have to take responsibility. Deciding meant taking responsibility, something I did not do well. I could manipulate well, but that was about someone else and it was up to me now.

The idea was so big it would overwhelm me if I did not have the great tools from the first and second stones. I could be powerless, and I could identify my unmanageability. I could see why I needed to work on the sanity. All this helped me understand that I could decide. Even if it was not the right decision, I could just reconsider the options and do it again.

To quote a Beatles song "Mother Mary came to me, let it be," which meant I could do it over and over. Music was a great part of my spiritual connection (my God). This was the God of my understanding, as it was my spiritual base. My God had no name, no specific religious sect, but an overall spirit of faith, comfort, and understanding. This worked for now. I could now use my spirit, which was alive again. I could love, feel, be emotional, hurt, cry, and be angry again. It was all about one day at a time and I could handle that.

My early decisions did not take place in my mind. I was not yet trusting of the way I thought. I felt more comfortable with my spirit, so the God of my understanding, and the decision to trust, was all about my spirit and my spiritual beliefs. **It's important that you sit back and take time and identify yours.**

Make decisions just for today.

Let's break it down. Make a decision for each category and list how you intend to carry out your decision. Who will it effect and why?

Family: _____

_____

_____

Money: _____

_____

_____

Friends: _____

_____

_____

Physical: _____

_____

_____

Mental: _____

_____

_____

Spiritual: _____

_____

_____

Other: _____

_____

_____

What are the decisions today that are too difficult to deal with?

_____

_____

_____

_____

If you turn them over what may happen?

_____

_____

_____

_____

Self-Will

Self-will means I want what I want when I want it. We have gone for so long abusing our right to make choices and make positive decisions. Self-will is the self-absorbed person we become. We exclude the feelings of others, the needs of others, and our responsibility to our family, employers, and the community. We manipulate all situations to meet our personal perceptions and aims.

We've thrown emotional tantrums and get our way. We are so busy achieving our obsessive and compulsive whims that we go off on tangents and fall flat on our faces repeatedly. We need to start identifying our self-will and make the decision to let the triggers go so we can move on.

What is self-will to you?

_____

_____

_____

_____

How do you act out on your own obsessiveness?

_____

_____

_____

What do you do when you don't get your way?

_____

_____

_____

_____

How do you feel once you manipulate to get your own way?

How are you going to change this attitude?

How has your self-will affected your family?

How has your self-will affected your physical health?

How has your self-will affected your spiritual health?

___

Self-destructive behavior is any behavior that is harmful or potentially harmful towards the person who engages in the behavior. Rather than deal with this fear, socially self-destructive individuals engage in annoying or alienating behavior, so that others will reject them first. More obvious forms of self-destruction are eating disorders, alcohol abuse, drug addictions, sex addiction, self-injury, and suicide attempts.

What are some examples of self-destructive behaviors you have exhibited?

___

Self-talk can have a great impact on your confidence. The effect can be good or bad, depending on whether your self-talk is positive or negative. It is worth the effort to practice talking positively to yourself, because the pay-off will be that you will feel better and your self-esteem will improve.

List some examples of positive self-talk in relation to yourself.

Setting goals and achieving them is crucial to your addiction recovery. When you attended a rehabilitation center, they teach you how to set recovery goals and then how to accomplish them. What is important is that when setting your goals, you be specific on exactly what it is you want to achieve. Making and setting goals is a healthy thing for every person to do but obsessive means of achieving these goals are negative.

Examples of Weak and Strong Goals

The following are examples of recovery goals. Each example will begin with a weak goal and a more specific recovery goal.

Example One

Meetings are very important for recovery. They are great places to get or give advice and meet new friends.

Weak Recovery Goal: I want to go to group meetings.

Specific Recovery Goal: I want to go to group meetings. I will do this by going every Friday and Saturday.

Example Two

You may have an addiction to some other substance such as cigarettes, soda, sugar, etc. You may feel a strong sense of satisfaction when you try to give up another dependency or addiction.

Weak Recovery Goal: Now that I am sober, I am going to quit smoking cigarettes.

Specific Recovery Goal: Now that I am sober, I am going to quit smoking cigarettes on Tuesday or I am only going to smoke 8 cigarettes a day, then I will gradually cut down and quit.

Example Three

Drugs and alcohol take away a lot of money; you will notice that once you are clean, you will have more money to do something that you have always wanted to do; like take a vacation.

Weak Recovery Goal: Now that I do not need drugs or alcohol, I will start saving money.

Specific Recovery Goal: Now that I do not need drugs or alcohol, I will start saving $100 a month by putting it into a savings account that I cannot get to easily.

Example Four

Spending time with your family is a great way to rebuild relationships or strengthen the ones that do not need rebuilding.

Weak Recovery Goal: When I was addicted to drugs or alcohol, I did not spend a lot of time with my family; now that I am sober I want to spend more time with them.

Specific Recovery Goal: Every Saturday will be family day; I will spend a few hours with my family. We will play games, go to the park, do some arts and crafts, etc.

Example Five

Exercise is very important for addiction recovery. It can help you to maintain a positive mood and boost your self-esteem.

Weak Recovery Goal: I'm going to exercise more.

Specific Recovery Goal: I will take a 30-minute walk on Monday, Wednesday, and Friday. I will do yoga and cardio on Tuesday and Thursday for one hour.

Writing the Goal

Try to write down at least a paragraph about what your goal is. How you are going to do it? Why it is important to you? The more details that you write down, the more you it will empower you to achieve it. Be sure to include every reason you can think of, even if it seems very small.

When you are writing down your goals, be sure that they are not too easy, but not too hard; find an in between. Make it something that you want and at the same time you know that with some will power and determination you can accomplish it.

Tips for Setting Your Recovery Goals

- Write it down;
- Don't just think of it in your head, instead write it down and read it on a constant basis;
- Be specific and detailed;
- Be as specific and detailed as possible but do not get lost in the small, unimportant ones;
- Visualize it;
- Visualize accomplishing your specific recovery goal; try to feel the joy an excitement that you will feel when you really do accomplish it;
- Challenge yourself;
- Challenge yourself, but don't set yourself up for failure; find a recovery goal that is right in between;
- Think positive; and
- Most importantly think positive, really believe that you can accomplish these recovery goals, and believe in yourself. Identify three personal goals.

Goal One: _____

_____

_____

_____

_____

Goal Two: _____

_____

_____

_____

_____

Goal Three: _____

_____

_____

_____

_____

Making and setting goals is a healthy thing for every person to do. However, obsessive means of achieving goals are negative. Can you identify past goals you made that were obsessive? How did it turn out?

_____

_____

_____

_____

How do you know when you are manipulating a situation or working towards a goal? Describe your interpretation of both.

_____

_____

_____

_____

At many points of recovery, we find ourselves turning back our old self-will attitude. After going back to, "My way or the highway," about recovery do we start dictating how other people should do things, hold on to things just a little too long (a feeling or emotional response), work too hard to get another person to see something our way, don't listen and want to talk all the time, and run out of patience, which causes us to seem to be a lot less humble and more judgmental.

By doing this we are shifting away from recovery. Our ego and self-will have come again to wreak havoc on our program and they will do so at will if not stopped immediately. If this is happening, you need to go back and redo the second and third stones.

If this happened to you explain your feelings.

_____

_____

_____

_____

How did you catch yourself?

_____

_____

_____

_____

How did you deal with the slip?

___

Reservations

Reservation is an unstated doubt that prevents you from accepting something wholeheartedly. It gives you an excuse to come back or repeat a negative thought or behavior (relapse). When we go to a hotel we make a reservation and that is to hold a room for us as we plan to use it upon arrival of a given time and date. Well, we do the same thing subconsciously when we reserve the right to relapse. When we bargain with our disease such as; "maybe after a while I can drink again", "I can still hang out, just not use", "I only go to the bar to play pool", "it's my sister so if she still uses pills that's not me", "after my probation or when all my court fines are paid and probation or DUI sanctions are met I can do anything I want as an adult". We tell ourselves that again we know how to do it better this time, so we go forward.

Have you really understood the concept of this program and that this is a disease?

___

What are the situations that I thought or convinced myself were acceptable to get high or drink over and when and why?

___

I know other people who now drink socially or smoke a joint occasionally. I believe I can also do this. Why?

_____

_____

_____

_____

_____

Do I believe with all the work I have done on myself I can now control my using?

_____

_____

_____

_____

How is this different from every other time you went back to thinking you had control over this disease?

_____

_____

_____

_____

_____

Surrender

<u>Surrender</u> means to relinquish the control over, not giving up in weakness but just being finished with the fight. When one army surrenders to another they refuse to fight any longer. When we surrender to the disease of addiction we are accepting that we cannot control this, and we just need to accept it.

It is a great mental relief to be done and look back at our definitions and see how powerless we are over our compulsive racing thoughts. What is the difference between resigning to a situation and surrendering? Well it's all about being done.

When I reserve a room, I don't own it. I just want to use it for a while but when I surrender I am finished. I own the responsibility for whatever reason I finally get it. I am ready to lay down my pride and my selfishness. I have no more fight in me. I put up my white flag and this is where my recovery begins.

I accept that I can never do it the same way. If I have failed before I now reserve the right to try again each time I surrender. I may not be sure of how to play this

New game of life but I know it will be by new rules. It's not about the game any longer, it's about me and what's important in my life.

To complete, determine if you understand this currently. It is important to sit down and write every possible reason or fear you can think of that keeps you from completely surrendering to the disease concept of addiction (friends, family, change, etc.).

_____

_____

_____

_____

_____

_____

_____

_____

This is a great place to do another inventory. Do this inventory using your categories and

GO TO: INVENTORY LOCATED ON PAGES 257-264

What would my life be like if I surrender to the concept that I have a disease and that it is about how I think?

_____

_____

_____

_____

What will my life and the life of the people I touch be like if I don't surrender, and continue the way I have been going with compulsive and obsessiveness of my thinking that dictates my actions?

_____

_____

_____

_____

At this point you need to see if you've only gotten sober or if you are ready to embrace recovery. Write your thoughts.

_____

_____

_____

_____

_____

Spiritual Power Revisited

Do you feel comfortable with the phase a "God of your understanding"? Let me give you my interpretation and see if it helps with your comfort zone. It is a personal, spiritual power that you have a relationship with. Its power is how it makes me feel and its ability to take from me, when I need it, the problems I cannot handle. It can be anything that speaks to you and gives you the feeling of safety and wellbeing.

Mostly, whatever the feeling or emotion is we can express it and feel better after. No magic, no lightning bolts, no separation of waters, just a way of developing trust in ourselves and a better understanding of ourselves through the clarity we get when letting go of thoughts that we have held on to with no outlets. The times when we need our higher power will vary from hard times to good times.

As we created the relationship, we created the communication. Sometimes we need to ask for help and what we are really doing is asking our spiritual awareness to bounce back our clarity, so we can make decisions. We will find that we deal with stress more gently because we can breathe, think, and move away from the drama. *As I understand mine, it evolves as I grow.*

What does the phase "God of your understanding" mean to you?

_____

_____

_____

_____

If you are struggling with this concept, why?

_____

_____

_____

Turning Things Over

What does that mean? First, we must admit we have a problem. Then we need to understand how powerless we are over the compulsive and obsessive part of our thinking. That takes us right back to Stone One when we realize that we do not need to be right and that our way does not work, which has been proven repeatedly by our repeated bad decisions and poor choices. Are you ready to surrender your will and try another way?

We must have the ability to develop some trust and understand that trust means we make mistakes. The problem for me was always wanting to retain a small part of control. I was willing to admit I have a problem with drugs, but I did not feel my whole life had to go on the chopping block. I thought, I could trust my higher power with something, but I was not turning over my check book. Letting go is hard to do. We need to examine if we can turn things over and if not, why?

What does 'Turning Things Over' mean to you?

_____

_____

_____

_____

Does letting go make you feel like a weak person, not wanting to face your problems? Why?

_____

_____

_____

_____

Self-Inventory Sheet

How will your life be changed if you turn over to your higher power many of the issues you cannot deal with now? Use the categories below to answer.

Family: _____

_____

_____

Money: _____

_____

_____

Legal: _____

_____

_____

Children: _____

_____

_____

Drugs and alcohol: _____

_____

_____

Sex: _____

_____

_____

Food: _____

_____

_____

School: _____

_____

_____

Death: _____

_____

_____

Other: _____

_____

_____

Look at the changes in your life since you started this manual. How is the process beginning to unveil?

_____

_____

_____

_____

_____

_____

Affirmation

At this point in the manual you need to create an affirmation. An affirmation is a statement asserting the existence or truth of something. It is about having confidence and accepting that a new journey has begun, and you are a participant, not the leader.

Example: it might be a prayer, a short saying, a made up saying, etc. Something you can start the day with and end each night with, something you can say to yourself when you need courage or help with your journey or even your choices or to help you move on in this workbook.

Affirmations are always positive. *Category examples: Hope, Faith, Trust, Honesty, Willingness, and, Freedom*

Create one for yourself.

_____

_____

_____

_____

_____

What you have learned from Stone Three?

_____

_____

_____

_____

_____

_____

_____

The Fourth Stone

Congratulations you have made it to the Fourth Stone! Get yourself a treat, take a break, and when you are ready let's begin!

The principals of truth and revelation are now required, and you are about to start the process of peeling away the old scales and exposing the truth in every light. We will be looking at the exact nature of our wrongs and how the use of alcohol and drugs was not the beginning, but rather the middle or end of a progression of bad decisions and choices that started long before.

Freedom waits for you at the end of this stone, but you must be ready for it. In other words, the journey is about to take a lot of turns, and you need to be able to take these turns and steep valleys mentally and emotionally. Whatever the force was, it is about to be opened and light is about to come into some dark areas. Are you ready? Let's see.

What is your biggest fear about the fourth stone?

_____

_____

_____

_____

What do you know about yourself that you are ready to expose and have not done so before in stone two or three?

_____

_____

_____

_____

What benefits can you take from this stone if you truly let go of the dark side of your secrets?

_____

_____

_____

Brave and Invasive

You need to make a brave and invasive compilation of your morals and values. <u>Brave</u> means ready to face and endure danger or pain; showing courage. <u>Invasive</u> means to search completely within you, leaving no stone unturned. Stop and look at all your work and decide if you are mentally and spiritually ready to move on. You need to have a solid understanding of this disease and while you are working this manual is a good time to stop, look, and listen to your spirit, heart, and mind in that order and write down your thoughts in your journal.

'<u>Brave and Invasive</u>', means go for it. Stop being afraid of the truth and allow the truth to set you free. Take the alternate risk and go ahead despite your fear and despite what others may think. Courage is about change and now we are about to change everything.

I want you to put this manual away for the day and do something you have never done before, be it whatever. If you have never ridden a Harley, go and try one out. If you have never gone horseback riding, it's a good day to do so. If you have never cooked without a recipe, make one up. Color your hair. Sing a song aloud, anything. Put away your safe mode, and experience taking a chance. The only way to conquer fear is to face it. So now is the time.

What are your most hidden fears?

_____

_____

_____

_____

_____

_____

_____

_____

_____

_____

What can you do to face them?

___

___

___

___

What if you make a fool of yourself?

___

___

___

___

What if you fail?

___

___

___

___

What if you succeed?

___

___

___

___

What if you made a promise and now need to break that promise?

_____

_____

_____

_____

This is where the rubber meets the road. If you have really learned to trust yourself, turned things over, and are ready to walk further on this journey than before, then it's time to go forward. If not, STOP here and go back to stones one, two, and three. Starting over will only give you more motivation and clear up more spider webs in your brain, heart, and spirit.

Talk about how you feel at this point.

_____

_____

_____

_____

_____

_____

_____

_____

_____

_____

_____

_____

Do not go on alone. Have a sponsor, a mentor or a teacher now involved. The truth is, being clean and sober can work against us if we do not take an inventory of our lives. You cannot allow the past to dictate your future.

What does this mean to you?

_____

_____

_____

_____

Remember all our fears stem from our life experiences. Know that you will be revealing destructive patterns and we cannot continue them.

Recognize some of your fears in the following categories:

Substance abuse: _____

_____

_____

Family: _____

_____

_____

Relationships: _____

_____

_____

Peer pressure: _____

_____

_____

Greed: _____

_____

_____

Ego: _____

_____

_____

Belief systems: _____

_____

_____

Sexuality: _____

_____

_____

Abuse Issues: _____

_____

_____

Resentments: _____

_____

_____

Others: _____

_____

_____

Are you still afraid of this stone?

___

Moral Compilation

The definition of moral is being concerned with the principles of right and wrong behavior and the goodness or badness of human character. Compilation is just a list. Most people have many unpleasant associations with the word moral. It brings out ugly thinking. It makes us think of others who see themselves as above us and still do painful and hateful things. These are rebellious times in our lives when we acted out in ways that disgust us now. You are as sick as your secrets and we choose to no longer to hold these secrets.

When you hear the word moral what do you think?

___

Recognize your morals and values in the following categories (Use feelings and emotions):

Dishonesty: ___

Battery on others: _____

_____

_____

Sex: _____

_____

_____

Lying: _____

_____

_____

Manipulating others, we love: _____

_____

_____

Abandonment of faith: _____

_____

_____

Others: _____

_____

_____

Can I discuss this with anyone else? Who and why?

_____
_____
_____
_____

Remember this is about you and no one else. Do not use another's moral compilation. This is your recovery, your journey.

Review of Spiritual Principles

Who do I still resent and why?

_____
_____
_____
_____

Do you resent local, state, and federal government?

_____
_____
_____
_____

What led you to these resentments?

_____
_____
_____

What repeats itself over and over in your compilation?

___

Reviewing Denial

Can you identify what you are still in denial about?

___

What are you still making excuses about?

___

What feelings are you denying?

Are you manipulating your feelings?

What do you do with the feelings you don't like?

What are you still trying to control after all the work you've done?

Guilt and Shame

Guilt is the fact of having committed a specified or implied offense or crime. Shame is a painful feeling of humiliation or distress caused by the consciousness of wrong or foolish behavior.

List some reasons you feel guilty?

_____

_____

_____

_____

List some reasons you feel shame?

_____

_____

_____

_____

Combining both lists, list the ones that are your own and ones you have taken on, which were never yours or ones you imagined?

_____

_____

_____

_____

What feelings of guilt do you own based on your past actions?

_____

_____

_____

We need only own what is ours and let go of what is not!

What in your life has created shame that you have never had any part in? Use the following two categories to answer:

Family: _____

_____

_____

_____

_____

Other people: _____

_____

_____

_____

Have you ever apologized for something that you never did? What was it? Why?

_____

_____

_____

_____

_____

_____

_____

Remember addiction is not just the use alcohol and drugs. It is obsessive compulsive behavior at all levels. We find so many fears from childhood and up. Now you can discuss them.

What were some of your childhood fears?

_____

_____

_____

_____

How did you mask your fears?

_____

_____

_____

_____

A <u>bully</u> is a person who uses strength or power to harm or intimidate those who are weaker.

What is a bully to you?

_____

_____

_____

_____

Does bullying have anything to do with your fear?

_____

_____

_____

_____

How do you respond to your fear, both positive and negative?

_____

_____

_____

_____

How have you cheated yourself with fear?

_____

_____

_____

_____

If you expose your fears and feelings what can you expect?

_____

_____

_____

_____

In the Fourth Stone we begin to look at your relationships, not only with partners but with all the factors of our internal and external families.

Let's discuss your relationships in the following categories and what you can do to strengthen them. Take a moment for each and list who they are, how they have been a part of your life, how long they have been in your life, and how you can strengthen the relationship. You can also include teachers, clergy, and even stores you frequent:

Work or school: _____

_____

_____

Significant others: _____

_____

_____

Children: _____

_____

_____

Parents: _____

_____

_____

Siblings: _____

_____

_____

People who play a role in our extended family and friends: _____

_____

_____

Grandparents: _____

_____

_____

Neighbors: _____

_____

_____

Higher Power: _____

_____

_____

Take each relationship listed above, one at a time, and explain their conflicts and benefits.

What influences from these relationships do you relate to most?

What patterns keep repeating themselves? (negative first, then positive)

What have you encouraged for your own selfish benefit in the relationships?

What have you sacrificed?

What are some of your relationship expectations?

How do you consider the feelings of others while still staying true to your own?

What are the problems due to culture or economics in the relationships?

What are your resentments in these relationships?

_____

_____

_____

_____

_____

What are some major achievements in these relationships?

_____

_____

_____

_____

_____

Now I want you to take the same list (relationships) and answer the following:

How do I change personalities in the relationship?

_____

_____

_____

_____

_____

Have I used or manipulated sex in the relationship, trying to control others?

_____
_____
_____
_____

After answering all the above, write a full essay on what you have identified. This will show you what each relationship means to you.

_____
_____
_____
_____
_____
_____
_____
_____
_____
_____
_____
_____
_____
_____

Now identify how you can grow from these relationships and what you must do next to ensure that growth.

_____

_____

_____

_____

_____

_____

Please do not do this next part alone. It is emotionally too dangerous. Have a mentor, teacher, or sponsor (not a partner) do this with you. After you begin, go through each phase slowly and if you're not ready, do not do it.

If you keep the dirty secrets about abuse you will never heal and be able to continue your journey. This path may need to be walked later in recovery when you feel more confident and trusting of the process.

"We are not to blame"

Have you ever been abused physically, sexually, mentally? Take each one separately and free write for a long as you need to. Lines are provided but continue in your notebook.

_____

_____

_____

_____

Have you ever told anyone before?

_____

_____

_____

_____

Is the abuser still part of your inner or outer circle?

_____

_____

_____

_____

How has being abused affected your relationships with your partner, family, children, work, school, etc.?

_____

_____

_____

_____

By writing and talking about this I can become whole.

Were you the victim or the abuser?

_____

_____

_____

_____

What were you feeling, if you were the abuser?

_____

_____

_____

_____

Did you blame your victim?

Did you protect your abuser?

Do you trust your higher power to give this up and move on with your life?

Do you now need to contact authorities?

Do you want to confront your abuser? What would you say?

_____

_____

_____

_____

_____

_____

_____

_____

Do you need to make amends to your victim? What will you say? How will you say it?

_____

_____

_____

_____

_____

_____

_____

_____

Are you ready to take whatever the consequences are?

_____
_____

Since the past sections have been about redirecting and making amends now I want you to look at your assets and really see what you have learned from the first four stones before moving to the fifth.

What is it now about you that you believe has made you a nicer more honest and commendable person?

_____
_____
_____
_____

What spiritual principals are you now living with?

_____
_____
_____
_____

How has your trust grown? In what ways?

_____
_____
_____
_____

How is your higher power working now in your life?

_____

_____

_____

_____

What goals in recovery have you accomplished? What goals are you going to set that you are ready to work towards?

_____

_____

_____

_____

_____

_____

What are your values now? How do they differ from before?

_____

_____

_____

_____

_____

_____

_____

_____

Let's look at the history of your addiction and do an auto-biography. This is going to use every tool you have learned to walk during first four stones. If you feel you do not have your balance yet you might want to go back to the beginning of the manual, hold your stone, look at all the questions and answers, and decide if anything needs to be expanded on.

Write your story from the beginning to now. Take as much time as you need. Some lines have been provided but the rest will need to be done in your notebook. Make it as long as you are able to write.

_____

_____

_____

_____

_____

_____

_____

_____

_____

_____

_____

_____

_____

_____

_____

_____

Now that you have written your story, what would you like to do with it?

Do you want to save the written work, why?

_____

_____

Who do you want to share this with and why?

_____

_____

How do you want to share your story?

_____

_____

What are your expectations?

_____

_____

Review and breathe!

Let's talk about sharing your feeling and apologies. Make a list of who you feel you are ready to express remorse and amends to.

_____

_____

_____

_____

_____

Who are you not ready to make amends with but might want to at a future date?

_____
_____
_____
_____

Do you have a plan on how to make amends? What are your ideas?

_____
_____
_____
_____
_____
_____
_____
_____

Are you ready for whatever happens?

_____
_____

Write about each of the categories below with a brief statement of understanding for each person you want to talk to. Be honest so you can be prepared.

Acceptance: _____

_____
_____

Rejection: _____

_____

_____

Indifference: _____

_____

_____

Anger: _____

_____

_____

Denial: _____

_____

_____

Stop, breathe, and reflect!

The Fifth Stone

You made it to the Fifth Stone! Congratulations!

You should only start this stone when you are ready and have worked hard on the balance of the Fourth Stone. Even if others are not ready, you should start this stone when you are comfortable with yourself. **It's time to get ready for a big leap of faith.**

This is not about making a confession, such as going to church. This is about finally getting the secrets out that make our lives unmanageable and giving us the freedom to move on. The idea of telling our secrets to another human being, feeling that spiritual connection, we bring out in each other, is one of the most empowering feelings we will ever know. No drug has ever taken you higher than this. Now that you have moved on from the Fourth Stone it is not time to panic. You are at a point where you can talk to other people without guilt or fear of being judged or put down.

The thing I worried about the most is that I would not be able to move on or that I'd start telling someone, such as my god of my understanding, about my progress in the Fourth Stone and I'd stop and realize I need to do this again. There was so much more I could write or talk about or maybe something I was not ready to talk about and need to remove from my work.

This is the perfect time to step back and redo your Fourth Stone. The Fourth Stone takes a long time, so you might want to go back and review your Third Stone as well and check your balance (self-confidence). The feeling of being able to communicate is a great feeling. At this point, you have walked through your fear of others knowing about your problems or about your actions. You have learned how you have hurt and disrespect others. This has brought you down a new road of understanding and if you feel comfortable then you are ready to move on. Let's answer some questions to be sure you are ready to move on.

Are you ready to read and/or share your answers from the Fourth Stone? Why or why not?

_____
_____
_____
_____
_____
_____
_____

How many times have you read/reviewed your Fourth Stone work? Are you feeling steady on your feet and ready to move on?

_____

_____

_____

_____

Who do you trust enough to read this? How did you decide you wanted to share this with this person?

_____

_____

_____

_____

Before you move on, you need to question yourself and decide if you want to do this.

What are some of your personal fears about sharing your feelings with those you have identified?

_____

_____

_____

_____

_____

_____

_____

How did you getting past the block and carry that forward to this point, which is all about sharing feelings?

_____

_____

_____

_____

_____

How do you use your spiritual understanding of higher power as a release, so you can share the issues at hand? (*Examples: prayer, meditation, spiritual awareness through reading*)

_____

_____

_____

_____

What exactly are you saying when you acknowledge your history of wrong doings?

_____

_____

_____

_____

_____

What does and doesn't belong to us has always been an issue for addicts. We are human. We blame ourselves for the myths and drama. We deny the damage our disease has created for others. We overreact and underreact sometimes to the same issues. Let's do an inventory of this so we have a clear understanding of what is ours and what is not.

Family: _____
_____
_____

Friends: _____
_____
_____

Work: _____
_____
_____

Community: _____
_____
_____

Siblings: _____
_____
_____

Money: _____
_____
_____

Others: _____
_____
_____

Now that the inventory is done, what is your observation? How will help you to separate what you need to own and what is not yours?

_____

_____

_____

_____

_____

_____

_____

_____

_____

_____

In the earlier stones we discussed the following main areas of growth:

- Denial
- Unmanageability
- Spiritual Principles
- Insanity

Think about the qualities you looked for in the person you chose to share your answers to your Fourth Stone with. Let's look at some qualities, that should be obvious. Some of the most important qualities should have been: 1. They have been in recovery a long time, 2. They have worked or understood recovery and sobriety, and 3. They can distinguish between them. You should feel completely comfortable talking to this person about confidentiality issues, and be able to ask them questions.

Who did you choose? _____

What do you think your identified person will get out of hearing of your experiences with this manual?

___

Will this help them in their recovery? How?

___

How will this experience make you a better person?

___

Why are you willing to trust this person?

___

What do you expect from this person?

_____

_____

_____

_____

How will this help new ways and directions in your relationship?

_____

_____

_____

_____

Do you have any fear of this hurting your relationship?

_____

_____

_____

_____

Are you willing to accept feedback from this person?

_____

_____

_____

_____

Go back to Stones Two and Three and revisit spiritual principles. Without reading your prior answers redo the questions in that section.

Please score each of the following categories from one to six, one being the lowest and six being the highest. *Example: Six meaning "I am truly open and accepting of this". One meaning "My way or the highway, I am not open to new ideas".*

Open-mindedness: _____

_____

Honesty: _____

_____

Willingness: _____

_____

Criticism: _____

_____

Courage: _____

_____

Others: _____

_____

Why are the sections in Stones Two and Three on spiritual principals so important? It is all about trust.

Review your path so far and summarize. This may be a good time to rereview Stone Two and Three. If in the sharing of this Stone you have addressed an issue which was extremely painful or brought up old uncomfortable feelings, it is the time to inventory the feeling and be sure that you do not leave yourself vulnerable.

GO TO: INVENTORY LOCATED ON PAGES 257-264

Stop if necessary after the inventory and go back to whatever you feel is pulling at you. Then, go for a walk, talk to a friend, go to a meeting, go to church, have ice-cream, just be nice to yourself. Remember how much you care about you. Review and summarize before moving on.

Summarize the feedback you got from the person you shared with.

Do not leave anything unsaid about your feelings. Write more.

Do you have a sense of self-acceptance? If not, this is the place where you start your manual again.

Before going on please address the following:

How has your relationship with your higher power improved or gotten more detached since doing a fifth stone and reviewing all the others. Or is this relevant?

___

___

___

___

Have your relationships with your friend, sponsor, or mentor now changed?

___

___

___

___

How do you feel about you?

___

___

___

___

<u>How the Past affects the Present: Negative Core Beliefs</u>

We have explored and discussed how different sorts of experiences can influence and shape how we view, and feel about, ourselves. Often, these are experiences that have occurred earlier in our lives. So, if these experiences happened long ago, why is it that we still see ourselves in a negative light today? After all, haven't we had adult experiences that are quite different from the ones we had as children? Yet, we might still hear, in our minds, what our parents or other people have said to us years and years ago. We might hear ourselves saying things like "This is not good enough," "You could have done better," "You are so stupid."

We continue to experience low self-esteem today, even when our current circumstances are different from those of our past, because they are our negative core beliefs. Negative core beliefs are the conclusions about ourselves we have arrived at when we were children or adolescents, likely because of the negative experiences we have had. For example, a child who was constantly punished and criticized may come to believe "I am worthless," or "I am bad." These thoughts are what we call negative core beliefs. To a child or young person, these beliefs seem to make sense during those experiences because they are probably unable to explore other explanations for what is happening to them. These negative core beliefs are thoughts that are usually deep seated, firmly held, and strongly ingrained in our minds. They are evaluations of ourselves and our worth or value as a person. These beliefs say, "This is the kind of person I am."

Here are some other examples of negative core beliefs:

- "I am stupid."
- "I'm not good enough."
- "I'm not important."
- "I'm unlovable."
- "I'm fat and ugly."
- "I'm unacceptable."
- "I'm good for nothing."
- "I am evil."

Protecting Ourselves: Rules & Assumptions

When we strongly believe these negative statements about ourselves, it is not surprising that we feel very bad about ourselves and experience strong negative emotions. While we were experiencing negative situations, and coming to these negative conclusions about ourselves, the human survival instinct was also in operation. To ensure our survival and to keep on functioning, we begin to develop assumptions, rules, and guidelines for how we live our lives that help protect our self-esteem. They aim to guard and defend us from the truth of our negative core beliefs.

We might develop rules such as:
- "I must be the best at everything."
- "I must never make any mistakes."
- "I must never show any emotion in public."
- "I must always do the right thing."

We might also develop assumptions such as:
- "If I ask for something I need, I will be put down."
- "No matter what I do, it will never be good enough."
- "If I can't control my food intake, I will never be able to control anything in my life."

Rules and assumptions can also be combined, for example:
- "I must do everything I can to gain others' approval because if I am criticized in any way, it means I am not acceptable."
- "I won't try anything unless I know that I can do it perfectly, because if I can't, it means I'm a total failure."
- "I have to always be slim and dress well, or else I will never be accepted."

What sorts of rules and assumptions for living do you have that help you feel better about yourself? Take a few minutes to jot these down.

_____

_____

_____

_____

_____

_____

_____

_____

_____

_____

_____

_____

_____

_____

_____

Rules & Assumptions Guide Behavior

The result of having these rules and assumptions is that they will guide your behavior. What you do on a day-to-day basis is largely determined by what rules for living you have. Makes sense, doesn't it? So, depending on your rules, you will try very hard to do everything perfectly, avoid getting too close to people, restrict your food intake and exercise vigorously to stay slim, do what it takes to please people, avoid doing anything too challenging, and avoid doing things you've never done before … and the list can go on.

Can you see how having such rules and assumptions for living might help you protect your self-esteem? What happens if one of your rules for living is "I must never make any mistakes?" The effect is that this rule will guide your behavior, making you become very careful about your work, checking your work many times so it is likely that you don't make many mistakes, if at all. This means that you are less likely to be criticized and so your self-esteem is protected.

Take a few minutes to jot down how your rules and assumptions might influence your behavior. What do you do to try to live up to your rules or standards and assumptions for living?

_____

_____

_____

_____

_____

_____

_____

_____

_____

_____

_____

What this means is that you can feel good about yourself if you are able to meet these rules for living or live up to the standards you have set for yourself. For example, if you can always maintain your body shape and weight, you will feel okay about yourself. If you never make any mistakes, always gain your friends', colleagues', or bosses' approval, always get extremely good results at school or university, you can maintain an adequate level of self-esteem. However, there is a disadvantage to having these rules and assumptions. You can run yourself ragged by trying to live up to all the rules. Basically, you are putting yourself under a lot of pressure so that you manage your self-esteem and don't feel bad about yourself.

While things might seem to be going well on the surface, the negative core beliefs are still there. This is because the negative core beliefs have not been removed. In fact, they are still there because they have been protected by your rules and assumptions and your behavior. Therefore, these rules and assumptions and your behavior cannot really be considered helpful because they serve to keep the negative core beliefs alive, as they were. At this point in time, if you have been able to live up to your rules, you may be feeling fine, but the low self-esteem lies dormant.

<u>Model of Low Self-Esteem: How Low Self-Esteem Begins</u>

As we go along, our discussions about how low self-esteem develops and what it keeps going will be put in the form of a diagram, which will tie everything together. We call all the concepts expressed in such a diagram a 'model'. We will begin with the concepts discussed in this Section and then add others in as we move on to the next Section. Here's the first part of the model of low self-esteem:

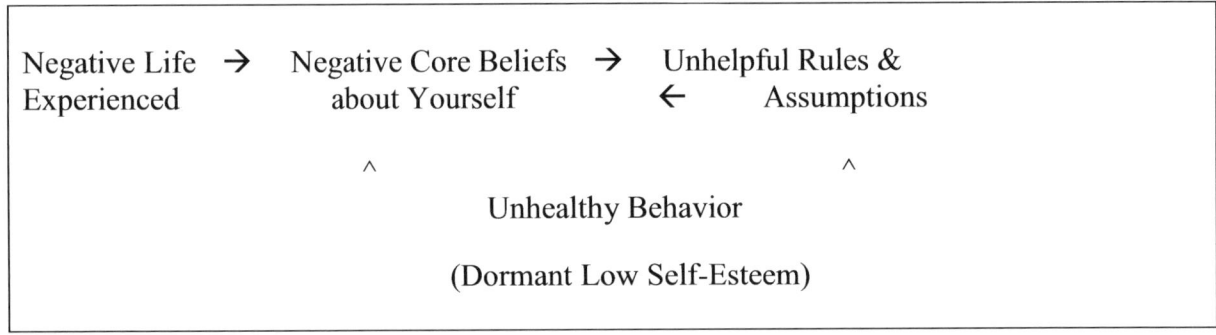

What this model depicts, is a snapshot of what has been discussed in this Section, Low self-esteem might begin with our having had negative life experiences, especially during childhood and adolescence. These negative experiences can influence how we see ourselves and we can come away with some negative conclusions about ourselves, which we call negative core beliefs. (The dotted arrow in the diagram signifies that negative life experiences do not automatically lead to negative core beliefs – it is just that they have some influence in their development). To protect our self-esteem and continue to function from day-to-day, we develop rules and assumptions for living. These rules guide us to behave in ways that end up not being very helpful because they serve to keep our negative core beliefs intact. While we can stick to these rules for living, we can feel okay about ourselves, but the low self-esteem remains dormant.

In the next Section, we will discuss what might cause low self-esteem to 'flare up' or be activated. We will also discuss many things that keep low self-esteem going.

How Low Self-Esteem Is Maintained

Introduction

Negative beliefs about ourselves can develop from past experiences. It is important to understand how and why we come to think about ourselves the way we do. To begin to tackle the problem of low self-esteem, it is also important to understand how negative beliefs about ourselves are maintained, that is, why these beliefs persist, long after the experiences that allowed them to develop have passed. In this Section, we will explore how negative beliefs about the self are maintained in the long-term.

How Negative Core Beliefs are Maintained from Day to Day

As you have seen, the negative beliefs we have about ourselves often have their roots in our early life experiences. Through various things that have happened to us and the way we interpret these events as a child or adolescent, we conclude that we are "stupid," "incompetent," "unlovable," "ugly," or some other negative judgement. That was then. However, now as adults, there are things we do on a day to-day basis that keep the negative beliefs we developed about ourselves in our early life, very much alive and well today. The way we make sense of information from the world around us, the things we do to live up to our unhelpful rules and assumptions, and particularly, our responses to certain day-to-day situations, all serve to keep our negative core beliefs going.

Information Processing

The way we make sense of the things that happen around us (we call this "information processing"), plays a very big part in maintaining low self-esteem. There is so much happening in our environment at any one time – so much information – that to deal with or make sense of all of it is an impossible task. For this reason, our brain tends to choose what we pay attention to and how we think about and make sense of things. Often, what determines what we pay attention to and how we think about these things, are the beliefs we hold. We tend to pay attention to things we expect and interpret things in a way that is consistent with our expectations. As a result, we tend to remember only things that happen in our lives that are consistent with what we believe to be true. This process of attending to and interpreting things in a manner that is consistent (rather than inconsistent) with our beliefs, is something all human beings do and not just those with problems with low self-esteem.

Let's look at this further using an example not related to self-esteem. For example, you may have the belief, "My neighbors are noisy." Now, this belief may be based on your experience of the first night they moved into the house next door and had a loud party that kept you awake all hours of the night and early morning.

However, your belief about your neighbors, which started from an initial experience, might remain a few years later because:

- You only pay attention to your neighbors at times when they are noisy, not at times when they are quiet
- You interpret any noise you hear as coming from those particular neighbors, often without checking if this is the case. Therefore, whenever the topic of your neighbors comes to mind, you only remember the occasions that they have been noisy.

Therefore, your original belief, "My neighbors are noisy" holds strong.

Let's try another example, but this time related to low self-esteem. Let's say that your negative core belief is "I'm a failure." This is a conclusion you arrive at following certain experiences you had when you were younger, but how does this affect your information processing now? Holding the belief, "I'm a failure," means that you probably only focus on the times you make mistakes or don't do something well. You probably ignore any successes, or play them down (e.g., "That was a fluke"). Also, it is unlikely that you acknowledge the times when you had done an acceptable job – those times are never given a second thought because to you they are "No big deal." Therefore, you only pay attention to negative incidents that confirm your belief that you are a "failure." You probably also have quite an extreme view of what success and failure is, with no middle ground. As such, words like "I did okay," rarely enter your vocabulary. You might easily jump to the extreme conclusion that you have failed at something, when realistically you might not have done too badly at all ("I didn't get an A on the assignment – I'm a complete failure!"). Therefore, you also tend to interpret the things that happen in your life as confirming your belief that you're a "failure" when there are likely to be other less harsh interpretations you could make.

The problem is that you seem to be always gathering evidence that supports your negative core belief, because you only ever pay attention to things and interpret things in a manner that confirms how you see yourself. In this way, your negative core beliefs are 'self-fulfilling.' Once they are in place, you will keep gathering information to keep them strong, and rarely gather information to challenge and expose them as biased and inaccurate opinions of yourself.

Unhelpful Rules & Assumptions Generate Unhelpful Behaviors

While the unhelpful rules and assumptions are designed to protect you from the truth of your negative core belief, these also play a part in keeping the core belief alive. Unhelpful rules and assumptions like, "I must do everything 100% perfectly, otherwise I will fail," or "If I get too close to other people, they will reject me" or "People won't like me if I express my true feelings and opinions," will tend to affect how you behave. You will run yourself ragged trying to do everything perfectly, or stay at a comfortable distance from others to avoid rejection, or not show anyone the true you in the hope that you will be liked. If you do these things, you will probably feel okay about yourself.

The problem is that these rules restrict your behavior in such a way that you don't get an opportunity to put your negative core beliefs to the test and see if they are true. You never intentionally do a mediocre job and see if dire consequences follow. You never get close to others to see if you really would be rejected. You never express your opinion and see if people still accept you. These rules make us behave in ways that are unhelpful to us. Essentially, they stop us from putting ourselves 'out there' to see if the things we believe about ourselves are true or to see if the consequences we fear are true. In this way, the rules, and assumptions we have limit our opportunities to have experiences that are inconsistent with our negative core beliefs. They restrict us from behaving in ways that allow us to have experiences that would challenge our beliefs and change them. Hence, the unhelpful behavior that is aimed at meeting our rules and avoiding our assumptions, also keep our negative beliefs about ourselves alive and well. In the previous Section, we mentioned that if we can live up to our rules and assumptions, we might not feel bad about ourselves, but the low self-esteem lies dormant.

At-Risk Situations

Life is full of all sorts of challenges every day. When these challenges relate to your negative core beliefs and unhelpful rules and assumptions, they become what we would call "At-Risk Situations" for low self-esteem. These are situations where your rules and assumptions are at risk of being broken or are broken outright (ex., you can't or will have great difficulty living up to your rules or avoiding your assumptions). Such at-risk situations are always going to arise because our rules and assumptions are unrealistic, extreme, and inflexible, and so because of the high and often impossible standards that have been set, these rules will always be susceptible to being broken.

What happens when we are faced with an at-risk situation? This is when the dormant low self-esteem becomes active. When you encounter an at-risk situation, your negative core belief about yourself is activated (i.e., it 'goes off' like an alarm, 'lights up' like a light bulb, is 'rekindled' like a burning flame) and influences how you think, behave, and feel in the situation. When a negative core belief is activated in an at-risk situation, you are likely to think that things will turn out badly or you become extremely critical of yourself. We call these two types of thoughts Biased Expectations and Negative Self-Evaluations, respectively. These types of thoughts will then influence how you behave. You might avoid doing certain things, try things out but quit when things get too difficult, take precautions to prevent a negative outcome, or withdraw from situations. These behaviors are unhelpful because they do not address the main issue or solve the problem. Instead, they lead to negative unhelpful feelings (such as anxiety, frustration, depression, or shame) and confirm the negative core belief. This also causes the negative core belief to remain activated and this time, the low self-esteem is no longer dormant – it is now acute low self-esteem.

Model of Low Self-Esteem: How Low Self-Esteem Is Maintained

Let's look at how these concepts fit together in our model and then we will further illustrate this with examples. In the previous Section, we presented the first part of the model. Here's the second part.

At-Risk Situations

Situations in which unhelpful rules & assumptions
Are under threat of being broken or are broken

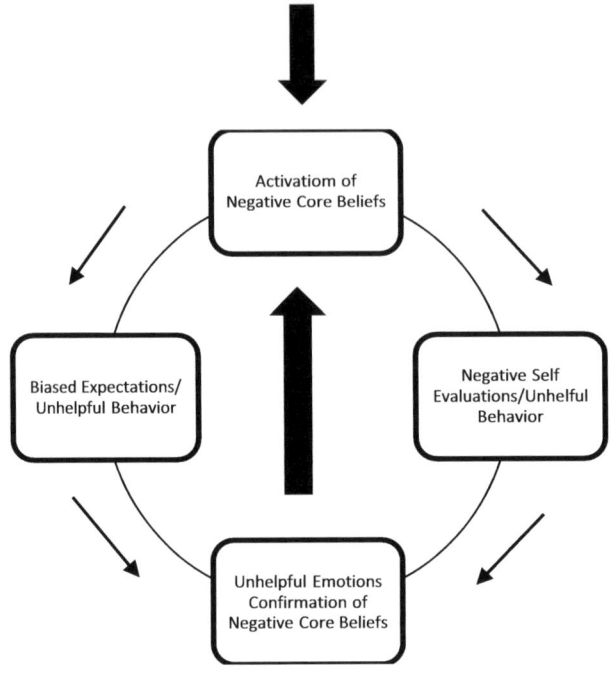

(Acute Low Self- Esteem)

Here's an example. Let's say that your negative core belief is, "I am incompetent," and your unhelpful rule is, "I must do everything 100% perfectly, without mistakes, and without the help of others." If you follow your rule, you might feel okay about yourself, because your incompetence is hidden for the time being. However, let's say you encounter a new and challenging experience – you are starting a new and difficult course of study. You are now in a situation where you are probably unable do things 100% perfectly, without mistakes or without the help of others, because the situation you are in is new and challenging, and you lack experience in this area. You are now in an at-risk situation for low self-esteem, because your rule is either broken or likely to be broken. When this happens, your belief, "I am incompetent," is activated, and this belief is brought to the forefront of your mind and now affects how you respond in the situation.

Biased Expectations

If your rule is only threatened (i.e. it hasn't been broken yet, but looks likely to be broken at some point), your response might be to expect that things will turn out badly. We call this having biased expectations. This means that the way you think is consumed by predicting the worst and jumping to negative conclusions about how the situation will pan out, saying things such as, "I'm not going to be able to do this," "I will fail," "Others will criticize me," "I won't do a good job."

Because of having these biased expectations, you might behave in certain ways. You might begin to avoid attending lectures or put assignments off until the last minute. You might become extremely cautious and over-prepared, such as staying up all hours of the night working on an assignment.

Alternatively, you might give the course a try but withdraw when an assignment seems too difficult. We call these three types of behaviors avoidance, taking safety precautions, and escaping. These thoughts and behaviors contribute to you feeling anxious, nervous, tense, afraid, uncertain, and doubtful. Your biased expectations, unhelpful behaviors, and anxiety may impair your performance, and confirm to yourself that you were right – "I am incompetent." Your negative core beliefs therefore remain unchanged and continue to be activated. By avoiding things or escaping from difficult situations, you never test out your biased expectations to see if they are accurate. Even if your biased expectations do not come true and things go well, by taking safety precautions, you might believe that everything is a "close call" this time, and that you might not be so lucky next time. Again, your negative core belief is not changed. So, you can see that the way you think and behave in at-risk situations leads to unhelpful emotions and maintains your negative beliefs about yourself.

Negative Self-Evaluations

If your rule is broken, your response might be to engage in negative self-evaluations. This means that the way you think is consumed by self-blame and self-criticism. You become very harsh on yourself, beating yourself up about perceived mistakes or inadequacies saying things such as, "I should have done better," "If I can't even do this, I must be really dumb," "I knew I didn't have it in me," "It just shows that I'm really lousy."

Again, as a result you may behave in certain ways, such as isolating yourself, withdrawing, hibernating, not taking care of yourself, not doing much, being passive, not doing enjoyable things – all because you think you don't deserve positive things.
When you think and behave in this way, you will tend to feel depressed, sad, low, upset, dejected, and hopeless. Given that a sign of depression is negative self-talk, these feelings will also tend to keep your negative beliefs about yourself activated.

What then happens is that your negative self-evaluations, unhelpful behaviors, and depression all confirm to you that you were right – "I am incompetent," and keep this belief alive, well after the at-risk situation has passed. So again, you can see that the way you think, behave, and feel in at-risk situations, means your negative beliefs gather further support and become even more unwavering.

Model of Low Self-Esteem: The Full Model

Let's put what we know from earlier sections together and get it clear in our minds how low self-esteem develops and is maintained. Here is the full model.

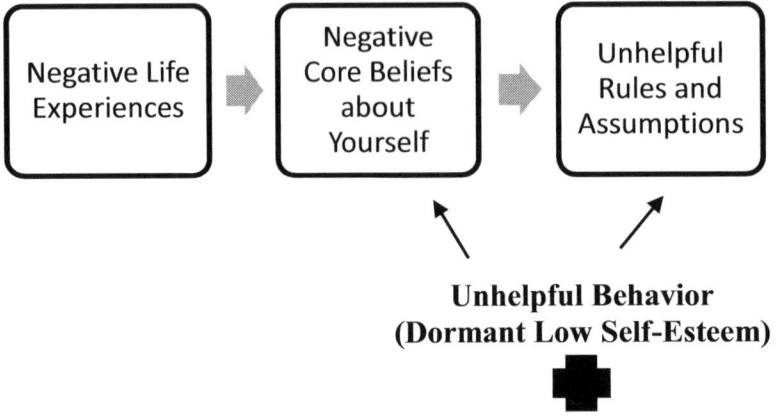

**Unhelpful Behavior
(Dormant Low Self-Esteem)**

+

At-Risk Situations

**Situations in which unhelpful rules & assumptions
Are under threat of being broken or are broken**

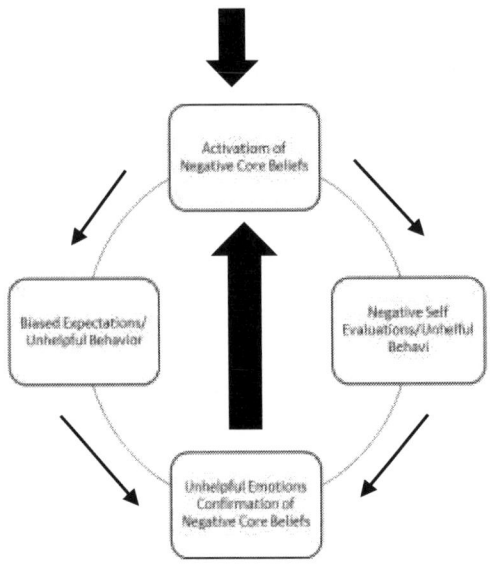

(Acute Low Self-Esteem)

This first part of the model shows that low self-esteem might begin with our having had negative experiences in our lives, which influence how we see and place worth on ourselves or aspects of ourselves. If we see ourselves in a poor light and place low worth on ourselves, it is likely that we have made some negative conclusions about ourselves, which are called negative core beliefs. To protect our self-esteem and continue to function from day-to-day, we develop rules and assumptions for living. These rules guide us to behave in ways that, in the end, are unhelpful because they serve to keep our negative core beliefs alive. While we can stick to these rules for living, we can feel okay about ourselves, but the low self-esteem remains dormant.

The second part of this model shows that at some point in our lives, we will encounter at-risk situations because it is extremely difficult to live up to our rules and assumptions, which are unrealistic and rigid. When these rules are at risk of being broken or have been broken, our negative core beliefs become activated and we engage in negative thinking. We expect that things will not work out (biased expectations) or criticize and blame ourselves (negative self-evaluations). We also engage in unhelpful behaviors and together with the unhelpful thinking, lead to negative unhelpful emotions and our negative core beliefs remaining activated. It is then that low self-esteem becomes acute.

The Good News

While it can be helpful to understand how the problems we have today might have developed from our past experiences, it might also be discouraging, because unfortunately we cannot change our past. However, what we have seen in this Section is that there are things we do on a day-to-day basis in the 'here-and-now' that maintain the negative core beliefs we have about ourselves, keeping them alive and active today.

This is good news, because given that these things happen daily, you can work on changing them. You can change the negative views you have developed about yourself. This means that things can be different, and you can overcome low self-esteem. What is important now is that you commit yourself to making the effort in addressing your unhelpful thinking and unhelpful behavior from day to day. The rest of the Sections in this package will focus on the things that you can start doing to chip away at your low self-esteem. Before long, you will begin to see yourself in a better light and treat yourself kindlier.

The approach taken in this information package of identifying and changing unhelpful thinking and behavior to overcome low self-esteem comes from a type of treatment known as cognitive-behavioral therapy. This type of psychological treatment has been evaluated scientifically and shown to be effective in treating many psychological problems. Cognitive-behavioral therapy is aimed at changing your unhelpful thinking patterns and beliefs (the cognitive part), as well as any unhelpful style of behaving (the behavioral part).

This will bring about a change in how you see yourself and how you feel.

The Sections in the remainder of this information package will focus on how to deal with biased expectations and negative self-evaluations first. The sections will then move to addressing unhelpful rules and assumptions, and finally negative core beliefs. You may ask why we do not start with negative core beliefs first, given that these are what determine how we think, feel, and behave from day to day. The reason we don't start with negative core beliefs is that these are a lot harder to shift than our thinking and behavior in daily situations. Examining our thinking and behavior in specific situations tends to be easier to do, so by starting here you can begin to get some immediate benefit for your efforts. Starting here can also have an effect of slowly chipping away at your negative core beliefs, and allows you to practice skills you will be applying to tackling your unhelpful rules and negative core beliefs later. So, we recommend that you work through this package in the order the Sections are presented (rather than skipping ahead), as this will bring the most benefit to you.

<u>Biased Expectations</u>

Introduction

Dormant low self-esteem becomes active and maintains itself until it becomes acute. When you encounter an at-risk situation, your negative core belief about yourself is activated and leads to two types of negative thoughts – biased expectations and negative self-evaluations. In this Section, we will examine biased expectations in more detail, and discuss ways of changing and overcoming them. By addressing your biased expectations in daily situations, you can prevent the negative beliefs you hold about yourself from being confirmed and re-activated. Ultimately, this will help you to chip away at your low self-esteem.

What Are Biased Expectations?

Biased expectations are negative thoughts that commonly occur when you encounter an 'At-Risk Situation' where it looks likely that your unhelpful rule or assumption will be broken, and your negative core beliefs have been activated. When this happens, you will tend to make predictions about how things will turn out and these predictions often tend to be negative. You will tend to:

- Overestimate the likelihood that bad things will happen
- Exaggerate how bad things will be
- Underestimate your ability to deal with things if they don't go well, and
- Ignore other factors in the situation, which suggest that things will not be as bad as you are predicting.
- When you jump to such negative conclusions about the future, you will tend behave certain ways – often engaging in unhelpful behaviors. You will tend to:
    - Avoid the situation totally,
    - Try the situation out but escape when things seem too difficult or the anxiety seems overwhelming
    - Be overly cautious and engage in safety behaviors. These are behaviors that you use to help you get through the situation. For example, you might take someone with you, over-prepare so that you can better face the situation, take medication to help you through, or place certain conditions on entering the situation (eg., turn up late/leave early).

At the end of the day, the unhelpful thoughts and behaviors contribute to you feeling incredibly anxious, nervous, uncertain, and unconfident about things – and this is confirmation that your negative core beliefs are true.

Here's an example of biased expectations in action. You can follow this example that is illustrated in the form of the model. Let's say that you have the negative core belief, "I am stupid." At present, your low self-esteem is dormant as you have developed the rule and assumption, "I must never let others see my true abilities, because if they do, they will know that I am stupid and not want to have anything to do with me." If you can live up to your rule, you might feel okay about yourself. However, the situation is about to change. A few of your friends invite you to join their team for a trivia night. You are now in an at-risk situation because you will have to show others your abilities at the trivia night. This means that your rule is likely to be broken.

At this point, you might have thought, "I'll be no good," "I'll let everyone down," or "Everyone will know how dumb I am," and are probably feeling anxious. It's also at this point that you could choose how to approach this situation. You could avoid the situation totally by declining your friends' invitation or you decide that you will accept the invitation. If you accept the invitation, you might then think about how you could make sure that people do not conclude that you are stupid. As such, you might prepare very hard for the trivia night by reading all the week's newspapers, watching current affairs programs and documentaries on TV, and reading trivia books. You might also think about how you could leave the trivia night half way through if things are not turning out well. As discussed above, all these are unhelpful behaviors, and they maintain your negative emotions and confirm your negative core belief.

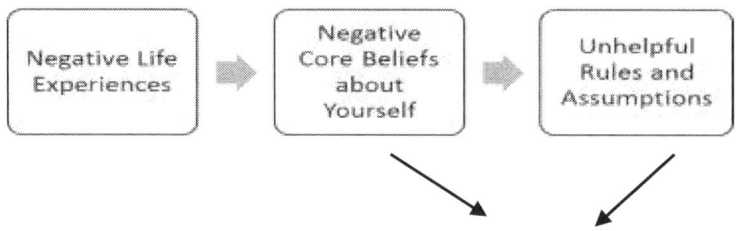

Unhelpful Behavior
**Say yes to all requests made to me
Bend over backwards to please people
Observe people carefully to see if they are ever displeased with me**

(Dormant Low Self- Esteem)

At-Risk Situation

Cancelled dinner with a friend because of work commitments

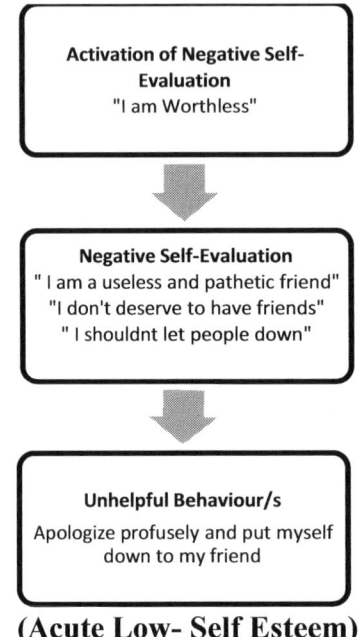

(Acute Low- Self Esteem)

Continuing with the above example, your belief "I am stupid" gets confirmed in many ways. Firstly, all the negative predictions confirm it you are making – all that 'negative self-talk.' Secondly, because you feel so anxious, you might use this as a sign that you are all the negative things you believe about yourself – "If I feel so anxious about this, I must be stupid." Thirdly, all your unhelpful behaviors mean that you are acting in a manner consistent with the idea that you are "stupid." So, if you act as if you are "stupid," you will continue to think and believe that you are "stupid." Finally, if things don't go the way you would like them to (eg, you get some of the questions wrong), you leave early. Because you do so, you don't give yourself a chance to answer a question correctly, or realize that getting a question wrong isn't such a bad thing, or just have fun regardless of the outcome. Alternatively, if things go okay and you answer a few questions correctly, you might ignore your efforts as "no big deal." If things go well and you answer heaps of questions, you might attribute it to all your preparation or say, "The questions were easy," but not acknowledge your own abilities.

What we have seen is an unhelpful way of responding to a daily situation, which helps keep your low self-esteem alive and well.

How could you respond differently, in a way inconsistent with low self-esteem?

_____

_____

_____

_____

How could you have realistic expectations and engage in helpful behavior?

_____

_____

_____

_____

Challenging Biased Expectations

One way to address biased expectations is to challenge them 'head on.' In cognitive behavioral therapy, this is also called 'disputation.' Remember that our thoughts and expectations are often opinions we have picked up or learned, rather than facts. Therefore, they can be questioned, and should not be something we just blindly accept if they are causing us distress.

To challenge or dispute your biased expectations means that you dissect them, evaluate how accurate or likely they are, examine what evidence you base your expectations on, and look at any positive things you may be ignoring. In this way, you are like a detective or lawyer, trying to get to the facts of how realistic your expectations are, and putting things in perspective.

Challenging your biased expectations isn't something you should do in your head as this can get messy and confusing. The best way is to write it down. To help you through the process, we suggest using a Thought Diary for Biased Expectations. This helps you work through the challenging process step by step, on paper, making things clearer and more helpful for you. On the next page is an example of how to complete a Thought Diary for Biased Expectations, and following that is a blank Thought Diary for you to practice on. The Thought Diaries guide you through how to get your biased expectations out on paper.

The Thought Diary will first ask you to Identify Your Biased Expectations. To help you do that, first ask yourself:

- What is the situation I am in?

Then:

- What am I expecting? • What am I predicting?
- What do I see happening in this situation?
- What conclusions am I making?

After you have written these down, you'll then need to ask yourself:

- How strongly do I believe this will happen? Rate the strength of your belief between 0
- and 100%
- What emotion(s) am I feeling?
- How intense are these emotions? Rate the intensity of your emotion(s) between 0 and 100%

Once you have completed the first section, you are ready to begin to Challenge Your Biased Expectations. Here are the questions asked in your Thought Diary to challenge these types of negative thoughts:

- What is the evidence for my expectations?
- What is the evidence against my expectations?
- How likely is it that what I am expecting will happen (Rate 0-100%)?
- What is the worst that could happen?
- What is the best that could happen?
- What is the most likely thing that will happen?
- How does it affect me when I expect the worst?
- If the worst did happen, what could I do to cope?
- How else could I view the situation?
- Are there any positives in me or the situation that I am ignoring?

The ultimate aim of doing this Thought Diary is for you to Develop more Realistic Expectations. Once you have explored the answers to the above 'challenging' questions in your Thought Diary, ask yourself:

- What would be a more realistic expectation?

The final step is then to:

- Re-rate how much I now believe the original biased expectation I was making,
- Re-rate the intensity of the emotions that I was originally feeling.

If you work through the entire Thought Diary for challenging your biased expectations, it is likely that you will experience a decrease in your belief in the negative predictions you were making and a decrease in the intensity of your emotions. Using a Thought Diary to develop realistic expectations will help quieten, rather than activate or confirm, your negative beliefs about yourself. This will help you approach situations with an open mind, try new things, and often be pleasantly surprised by what you find, instead of letting your negative opinion of yourself constantly interfere with how you live your life.

Try using a Thought Diary for Biased Expectations the next time you notice when you start feeling anxious, nervous, and uncertain, or doubt yourself and your abilities. Stop yourself when you notice these sorts of feelings, and see if you can find any biased expectations that are contributing to the feeling. See if you notice any predictions you are making, negative conclusions you are jumping to, or bad outcomes you are envisaging. If you notice these biased expectations rearing their ugly head, use a Thought Diary to tackle them. Continue to use a Thought Diary to deal with these sorts of thoughts and feelings, until it becomes second nature. Then, you will find that you can easily catch the biased expectations in your head and challenge them in your head. This will take some time and a lot of practice, so for now, stick to writing it all down in your Thought Diary.

<u>Thought Diary for Biased Expectations</u>
<u>Identify Your Biased Expectation</u>

What is the at-risk situation?	**How much do I believe it will happen (0-100%)?**
What am I expecting? What am I predicting? What do I see happening in this situation? What conclusions am I jumping to?	**What emotions am I feeling?**

Challenge Your Biased Expectations

What is the evidence for my expectations?	**What is the evidence against my expectations?**
How likely is it that What I am expecting will actually happen (0-100%)	
What is the worst that could happen?	**What is the best that could happen?**
What is most likely to happen?	**How does it affect me if I expect the worst?**
If the worst did happen, what could I do to cope?	
How else could I view the situation?	
Are there are any positives in me or the situation I am ignoring?	

Develop Realistic Expectations

What's a more realistic expectation?	
How much do I believe my original biased expectation now? (0-100%)	**How intense are my emotions now? (0-100%)**

Experimenting with Biased Expectations

By challenging your biased expectations as you did in the last section (using a Thought Diary), you can now be in a better position to approach situations with an open mind and with more realistic and balanced expectations. The next step of challenging biased expectations is to test them out to see how accurate they really are. This is like a scientist doing an experiment with your biased expectations, to test how true they are.

As with a Thought Diary, there are some steps you must work through to properly experiment with your biased expectations. Below is an example of how to do this.

Step 1: Identify Your Biased Expectations

From the first section of your Thought Diary, you will already know what the at-risk situation is and what it is that you have predicted in this situation, and how much you believe it will happen. Also, write down specifically how you will know if your biased expectations have come true. Ask yourself: *What exactly would happen? What would an outsider see happening? What would you be doing? What would others be doing?*

The Situation: **Friends invite me to be on their trivia team**
My Biased Expectations: **I'll be no good; I'll make them lose; I'll make a complete fool of myself; Everyone will see how dumb I am; The others will wish I wasn't on their team**
How much do I believe it will happen (0-100%)? **80%**
How will I know it has happened: **I won't know a single question. Everyone except me will know the answers. The others will make rude comments or glare at me.**

Step 2: Identify Your Unhelpful Behaviors

Next you need to identify what unhelpful behaviors you might be engaging in to cope with your negative predictions and anxiety (e.g., avoidance, escape, safety behaviors).

Over-preparing for the trivia (e.g., news, newspapers, trivia books), placing conditions on going (ex. planning to only answer if I am 100% sure), having an escape plan.

Step 3: Remember Your Realistic Expectations

Next remind yourself of the new perspective that you developed from your Thought Diary, as you will also want to test your new realistic expectations against your old biased expectations.

I don't have to be good, it's just a trivia night. They are my friends, they are just there to have fun and don't really care about winning or who answers what. It's likely that I will be able to answer some questions that are in my area of interest. How I do at a trivia night isn't a reflection of who I am as a person – everyone has their strengths and weaknesses.

Step 4: Identify Your Helpful Behaviors

This involves noting what it is you will do differently to test out your new and old expectations, to see which is more accurate. This is really setting up the experiment and specifying what it is you will do. This will generally involve confronting rather than avoiding the situation, staying in the situation rather than escaping, and stopping safety behaviors to see how you go by yourself and without imposing conditions and restrictions on you entering the situation.

> *Ask my friends if they are doing anything to prepare for the trivia night. If they do any preparation, do only as much as they are doing. If they are not preparing at all, go to the trivia night, without preparing beforehand. Stay at the trivia night until the end, regardless of how I am going with answering the questions. Answer questions even if I am not certain. Purposely suggest an answer that I know is wrong.*

Step 5: Carry Out the Experiment

Follow through with what you set out to do in Step 4. Carry out the experiment, engaging in the more helpful behaviors you have identified, and see what happens.

Step 6: Evaluate the Results

The last step is to reflect on what happened and how this compares to what you were expecting in Step 1. What were the results of the experiment? What did you observe? How does this compare to your biased expectations? Which expectations did the results support (biased or realistic)? What was it like to carry the experiment out and act differently? What did you learn from the experience?

What happened? *I answered some questions that were in my areas of interest. I got some questions wrong, but so did others – no one saw it as a big deal. I had a good time. No one seemed to take it too seriously. They seemed to be pleased to have me on their team.*
How much did my biased expectations come true (0-100%)? **10%**
Which expectations were supported by the experiment? *My more realistic expectations.*
What was it like to act differently? It was hard at first. But not over preparing, purposely suggesting a wrong answer, and not planning how to escape showed me that I can do this, and that not knowing everything is not so bad.
What did I learn? *This shows me that what I predict will happen in situations may be guided by my opinion of myself, and may not always be true. So I may need to make my expectations more realistic, act accordingly, and see what happens.*

If the results of your experiment do not support your biased expectations, which is often the case, that is great! It will be important to remember that the next time you find yourself making biased expectations. It will also be important to reflect and ask yourself "What does this mean for you as a person?"

However, should your biased expectations be supported, which may happen at times, it will be important to ask yourself some questions about this. Ask yourself: Were there are any other reasons for the result, aside from who you are as a person? *What else was happening at that time? Are there other ways of viewing what happened? What could you learn from the experience to improve or change things in the future?*

It is important to note that not everything we think is inaccurate, or has no grain of truth to it. However, often when we have problems with low self-esteem, we predict negative things about ourselves and our abilities all the time, and act accordingly. We never step back to question these predictions or test them out. This is a habit that is important to break. It is the automatic process of predicting the worst, because of our negative view of ourselves that we want to change. It is important to tackle this because if you can make more realistic predictions in your day-to-day life, you will think and act differently, in a manner inconsistent with someone with low self-esteem. Behaving in a manner that is inconsistent with your low opinion of yourself, is the path to overcoming this negative opinion. When you do this, you will start to gather new information about yourself, which will allow you to see yourself in a less harsh, more positive, and kinder light.

Now, it's time for you to do an experiment. Use the worksheet on the next page to help you plan an experiment to test out your biased expectations.

<u>Experiment Record for Biased Expectations</u>
<u>Step 1: Identify Your Biased Expectations</u>

The Situation:	
My Biased Expectations:	
How much do I believe it will happen (0-100%)?	
How will I know it has happened?	

Step 2: Identify Your Unhelpful Behaviors

Step 3: Remember Your Realistic Expectations

Step 4: Identify Your Helpful Behaviors & Set Up Your Experiment

Step 5: Carry Out the Experiment (from Step 4)

Step 6: Evaluate the Results

What happened?
How much did my biased expectations come true (0-100%)?
Which expectations were supported by the experiment?
What was it like to behave differently?
What did I learn from this experiment?

Negative Self-Evaluations
Introduction

Dormant low self-esteem becomes active and maintains itself until it becomes acute. When you encounter an at-risk situation, your negative core belief about yourself is activated and leads to two types of negative thoughts – biased expectations and negative self-evaluations.

By addressing your negative self-evaluations in daily situations, you can prevent the negative beliefs you hold about yourself from being confirmed and re-activated. Again, this will help you to chip away at your low self-esteem.

What Are Negative Self-Evaluations?

Negative self-evaluations are negative thoughts that commonly occur when you encounter an 'At-Risk Situation' where your unhelpful rule or assumption is broken, and your negative core beliefs have been activated. When this happens, you will tend to evaluate yourself in a negative way, becoming harsh and critical of who you are as a person. You will tend to:

- Tell yourself that you "should" have done this or "shouldn't" have done that, chastising yourself and beating yourself up, for not meeting the standards you have set for yourself
- Put negative and derogatory labels on yourself, calling yourself hurtful names like "pathetic," "useless," "idiot," and
- Make over-generalizations about yourself, based on a very specific event, saying things such as "I am always doing this," "I never learn," "Everything is ruined."
- When you are so critical of yourself, you will tend to tend behave in particular ways – often engaging in unhelpful behaviors. You will tend to:
- Withdraw or isolate yourself from family or friends,
- Try to overcompensate for things,
- Neglect things (opportunities, responsibilities, self-care), or
- Be passive rather than assertive with others.

At the end of the day, the unhelpful thoughts and behaviors contribute to you feeling depressed, low, sad, guilty – and this is confirmation that your negative core beliefs are true.

Here's an example of negative self-evaluations in action. Let's say that you have the negative core belief, "I am worthless." At present, your low self-esteem is dormant as you have developed the rule and assumption, "I must make everyone else happy to be accepted." If you can live up to your rule, you might feel okay about yourself. However, the situation is about to change. You have had to cancel dinner with a friend because of work commitments. You are now in an at-risk situation because you have disappointed someone. This means that your rule has been broken.

At this point, you might have thought, "I'm a useless and pathetic friend," "I don't deserve to have friends," or "I should not let other people down," and are probably feeling sad, depressed, and guilty. It's also at this point that you could choose how to behave in this situation. You could apologize profusely and put yourself down to your friend. You could try to make up for cancelling the dinner by offering to pay for the next outing or re-scheduling your dinner to a time that suits your friend but is inconvenient to you. This is overcompensation. Alternatively, you could withdraw from your friends for a while and avoid their calls and emails. All these are unhelpful behaviors, and they maintain your negative emotions and confirm your negative core belief.

Continuing with the example, your belief, "I am worthless," gets confirmed in many ways. Firstly, all the negative self-evaluations confirm it you are making – all that 'negative self-talk.' If you keep telling yourself these negative things, you will continue to believe them. Secondly, feeling depressed can confirm your belief that you are "worthless," because a symptom of depression itself is thinking negatively about everything, including yourself. Thirdly, all your unhelpful behaviors (ex., acting in a passive and apologetic way, trying to overcompensate, or withdrawing) mean that you are acting in a manner consistent with the idea that you are "worthless." So, if you act as if you are "worthless," you will continue to think you are "worthless," and feel sad or depressed.

It is important to note that some people think that making negative self-evaluations is a good thing. Some people think that:

- Being critical and harsh on yourself keeps you grounded
- It stops you from getting too big for your boots
- It prevents you from becoming a 'tall poppy' that needs to be 'cut down'
- It spurs you on, motivating you to do better and better.

Some of these might be commonly held beliefs, but are they true?

Is putting yourself down and criticizing yourself a good and healthy thing to do? If it is, then we would do it to our loved ones regularly. When something goes wrong and our loved ones are in distress, would we help them through by abusing them, calling them names, and telling them off? Is this what we do to the people we love?

Most people would probably not agree. Most people would say that they do the exact opposite – that when times are tough, they show compassion and kindness to the ones they love, comforting them and encouraging them. So, if this is what you would do for other human beings, why is it that you don't do it for yourself?

Take a moment to think about this issue of whether being harsh and critical of yourself is a healthy or unhealthy thing to do? Perhaps write down the costs of making negative self-evaluations. Note the disadvantages of being so critical of yourself. Think about how talking to yourself in such a harsh manner affects you? Does it prevent you from doing certain things? Does it make you feel a certain way? Is it unfair to yourself in some way?

Hopefully you are coming to see that constantly making negative self-evaluations is not only generally unhelpful, it also helps keep your low self-esteem alive and well. So how could you respond differently, in a way that is inconsistent with low self-esteem?

Challenging Negative Self-Evaluations

As we did with biased expectations, one way to address your negative self-evaluations is to challenge them, and develop balanced self-evaluations. Remember that our thoughts and evaluations are often opinions we have, rather than facts. Therefore, they are open to question, and should not be something we just blindly accept if they are causing us distress. Instead, you can dispute, dissect, examine, and assess them – like a detective or lawyer would, to see how realistic they are and put things in perspective.

Again, challenging your negative self-evaluations isn't something you should do in your head as this can get messy and confusing. The best way is to write it down. To help you through the process, we suggest using a Thought Diary for Negative Self-Evaluations. This helps you work through the challenging process in a step-by-step way, on paper, making things clearer and more useful for you.

On the next page is an example of how to complete a Thought Diary for Negative Self-Evaluations, and following that is a blank Thought Diary for you to practice on. The Thought Diaries guide you through how to get your negative self-evaluations out on paper and challenge them.

The Thought Diary will first ask you to Identify Your Negative Self-Evaluations. To help you do that, first ask yourself:

- What is the situation I am in?

Then:

- What am I saying to myself?
- How am I evaluating myself?
- How am I putting myself down?
- How am I criticizing myself?

After you have written these down, you'll then need to ask yourself:

- How strongly do I believe these evaluations of myself? Rate the strength of my belief between 0 and 100%
- What emotion(s) am I feeling?
- How intense are these emotions? Rate the intensity of my emotion(s) between 0 and 100%
- What unhelpful behaviors did I engage in?

Once you have completed, you are ready to begin to Challenge Your Negative Self Evaluations. Here are the questions asked in your Thought Diary to challenge your negative self-evaluations:

- What is the evidence for my evaluations?
- What is the evidence against my evaluations?
- Are these opinions I have of myself or facts?
- How helpful is it for me to evaluate myself in this way?
- How else could I view the situation? What are other perspectives might there be?
- What advice would I give to a friend in this same situation? • Are there any positives in me or the situation that I am ignoring?
- What would be more helpful behavior I could carry out?

Note. If you have engaged in any unhelpful behaviors, ask yourself: How could I act differently? How could I behave in a manner that is inconsistent with my negative self-evaluations? For example, instead of withdrawing and isolating yourself, be active and a part of things around you; instead of overcompensating for things, just do what you think the average person might do in this situation; instead of neglecting things, make time for them; and instead of being passive, try to be more assertive.

The aim of doing this Thought Diary is for you to develop more Balanced Self-Evaluations. Once you have explored the answers to the above 'challenging' questions in your Thought Diary, ask yourself:

- What would be a more balanced self-evaluation to replace my negative self-evaluation?

The final step is then to:

- Re-rate how much I now believe the original negative self-evaluations I was making,
- Re-rate how intense I now feel the emotions that I was originally feeling.

If you work through the entire Thought Diary for challenging your negative self-evaluations, it is likely that you will experience a decrease in your belief in the evaluations you were making and a decrease in the intensity of your emotions. Using a Thought Diary to develop balanced self-evaluations will help quieten rather than activate or confirm your negative beliefs about yourself. This will help you approach situations with an open mind, rather than letting your negative opinion of yourself constantly interfere with how you live your life.

Try using a Thought Diary for negative self-evaluations the next time you notice yourself feeling down, sad, depressed, guilty, or hopeless, and you have the sense that you are beating yourself up, being hard on yourself, telling yourself off, and criticizing yourself and your abilities. Stop yourself when you notice these sorts of feelings, and see if you can find the specific negative self-evaluations that are influencing your feelings. When you find these, use a Thought Diary to tackle them. Continue to use a Thought Diary to deal with these sorts of thoughts and feelings, until it becomes second nature. Then you will find that you can easily catch the negative self-evaluations in your head and challenge them in your head. This will take some time and a lot of practice, so for now, stick to writing it all down in your Thought Diary.

Thought Diary for Negative Self-Evaluations
Identify Your Negative Self-Evaluations

What is the at-risk situation?	How much do I believe these evaluation of myself (0-100%)?
What am I saying to myself? How am I evaluating myself? Putting myself down? Criticizing myself?	What emotion(s) am I feeling? (Rate the intensity 0-100%)
What unhelpful behaviors did I engage in?	

Challenge Your Negative Self Evaluation

What is the evidence for my evaluation? What is the evidence against my evaluation?
Are these options I have of myself or facts?
How helpful is it for me to evaluate myself in this way?
How else could I view the situation?
What advice would I give to a friend in the same situation?
What would be more helpful behavior I could carry out?

Balanced Self-Evaluations

A more balanced evaluation of myself is:	
How much do I believe my original negative self-evaluation now (0-100%)?	How intense are my emotions now (0-100%)?

As a preview, the next Section can be thought of as complementing the present Section. In the present Section, we have looked at how to quash your negative self-evaluations, allowing you to be less harsh and critical of yourself. The next Section also tackles this tendency to be very hard on yourself, but we will take a different route. Instead of trying to combat negative self-evaluations, we will look at how to promote balanced self-evaluations by paying attention to the positives aspects of yourself and treating yourself kindlier. Therefore, this and the next Section go hand in hand, working together to tackle our automatic tendencies to evaluate ourselves in a negative way.

Accepting Yourself
Introduction

Battling against some of the negative things you say to yourself is one path to overcoming low self-esteem. However, another path is to promote balanced evaluations of yourself. This means noticing and acknowledging the positive aspects of yourself, and behaving like someone who has positive qualities and is deserving of happiness and fun. In this Section, we will show you exactly how to go about doing these things to boost your self-esteem.

Focusing on the Positive You

Very quickly, jot down a few of your positive qualities in the space below, and then read on.

___

___

___

How easy was it for you to do that? Some people might struggle to bring things to mind. This is because, as we mentioned in earlier Sections, when you have low self-esteem, you tend to only pay attention to negative things that confirm your negative view of yourself. You rarely pay attention to the positive things you do, your positive qualities, positive outcomes, or positive comments from others. This will make the positive aspects of you very hard to get to at first, because you have not taken any notice of them. Other people might have less trouble recalling positive things about themselves, but instead might feel uncomfortable thinking about, talking about, or writing about the positive qualities they have. They might consider it as being conceited, arrogant, or stuck up to think about such things.

If either of these apply to you, you will need to approach this Section with an open mind. In this Section you will be asked to start noticing the positives in you that you often ignore and acknowledge these positives. Remember, most of the time all you pay attention to are your negative qualities and you feel comfortable dwelling on these negatives. Ask yourself how fair that is. By getting you to begin acknowledging your positives, you are really tipping the scales of self-evaluation back into balance. These scales have been off balance (towards the side of negativity) for some time now.

Positive Qualities Record

So, where do we start? When we notice something and it's important for us to remember it, what is it that we do to help us remember? We write things down, make a note of it, or make a list if there are many items. The same approach applies here. To start acknowledging your positives, you need to write them down.

What was your initial reaction to this suggestion of writing a list of your positive attributes? Did you feel any anxiety, shame, uneasiness, sadness, fear? Did you think "What could I possibly write?" "I have nothing worth writing down," "Me! Positive attributes? Ha!" You need to be careful here, and listen out for negative self-evaluations coming through, and the tendency you may have to discount or minimize anything positive about yourself. Remember that this is a nasty habit that may rear its head when you try to do this exercise. Should this happen, just acknowledge it, and try to move on to the task at hand. If the negative self-evaluations simply won't release their grip on you that easily, then go back to the Thought Diary for Negative Self-Evaluations to help you out.

Now, start a 'Positive Qualities Record.' Make a list of the positive aspects of yourself, including all your good characteristics, strengths, talents, and achievements, and record them on the worksheet. You might want to record all of this in a special book or journal – one that is dedicated especially to this task of focusing on your positive qualities.

Here are some important tips for getting started:

When you are recording something in your Positive You Journal, make sure you set aside a special time to commit to the task and carry it out. Don't do it on the run, or while you are doing other things, or fit it in around other activities. Instead, give it the due attention and time it deserves.

Remember to write them down on the worksheet provided or in your special journal, rather than just making a mental note or writing something on the back of a napkin or scrap of paper. Write your positive qualities in your journal or worksheet so that you remember it and know exactly where to find it. In this way, the positive qualities won't get lost.

Write as many positive things about yourself as you can think of…there is no limit. Exhaust all avenues and brainstorm as many ideas as possible. If you run out of steam, take a break. Come back to it over the course of a few days, until you have a substantial list of your positives.

Get help if you feel comfortable to do so. Enlist the help of a trusted friend or family member – someone whom you know would be supportive of you doing this, rather than someone who may be a contributor to your self-esteem problems. Two heads are better than one and an outsider might have a different perspective of you, than you do of yourself. Who knows what nice things you might discover about yourself with their help.

As already mentioned, watch out for negative self-evaluations or discounting your positives as "small" or "no big deal" or "not worth writing." You tend to remember detailed negative things about yourself, therefore we must do the same with the positives – it is only fair! Also remember, you don't have to do these positive things perfectly or 100% of the time – that is impossible. So be realistic about what you write down.

For example, if you tend to be 'hardworking,' but recall the one time you took a sick day after a big weekend, you might say to yourself "I can't write that down because I haven't done it 100%." If you take that attitude, you are not being fair and realistic with yourself.

Finally, don't just do this exercise for the sake of it, and then put it in the back of a drawer, never to be seen again. It is important that you re-read the things you write in your journal, reading them over and over with care and consideration. Reflect on what you have written at the end of the day, week, or month. Let all the positive qualities pile up and 'sink in.' this is important so that you learn to take notice of these things and feel more comfortable acknowledging them, rather than just giving them lip-service.

Listing the positives:

Now, let's get you started writing down all your positive qualities. Use the worksheet to help you start writing down all the positive aspects of yourself. If you get stuck, the worksheet has some questions that can help you jog your memory. Ask yourself questions like:

What do I like about who I am?
What characteristics do I have that are positive?
What are some of my achievements?
What are some challenges I have overcome?
What are some skills or talents that I have?
What do others say they like about me?

What are some attributes I like in others that I also have in common with?
If someone shared my identical characteristics, what would I admire in them?
How might someone who cared about me describe me?
What do I think are bad qualities?
What bad qualities do I not have?

*Remember to include everything no matter how small, insignificant, modest, or unimportant they are!

After using these questions to identify your positive attributes, your list may look something like this (of course everyone's list will be different, as we are all different individuals with different positive qualities):

Considerate	Good Listener	Diligent
Good Cook	Reliable	Good Humored
Fun	Helpful	Health Conscious
Well-Travelled	Animal Lover	House Proud
Resourceful	Adventurous	Loved
A Good Friend	Avid Reader	Charitable
Movie Buff	Politically Conscious	Artistic
Creative	Active	Outdoors Person
Strong	Friendly	Responsible
Determined	Organized	Appreciative
Praise Others	Cultured	

<u>'Positive You Journal'
Part 1: Remember Past Examples</u>

Using the worksheet, recall specific examples of how you have demonstrated each of the positive attributes you have listed in the Positive Qualities Record. This way, you will make each attribute you have written not just meaningless words on a page. Instead, each attribute will become a real, specific, and detailed memory of something that happened. So, for example:

Considerate

1. I took my friend some flowers and a book when they were sick.
2. I offered a listening ear to my colleague who was going through some difficult times.
3. I lent my brother some money when he was down on his luck.

Doing this will take some time, but is well worth the effort. Remembering the specific incidents that illustrate your positive qualities will allow the list to have an impact on your view of yourself, making it real.

Part 2: Noting Present Examples

Once you have spent time recalling past examples of your positive qualities, it is now time to turn to recognizing examples of your positive attributes daily. Use the worksheet to help you do this. This will be an ongoing exercise – something you do every day. Each day, set out to record three examples from your day, which illustrate certain positive qualities you have. Write exactly what you did and identify what positive attribute it shows in you. Here's an example:

Day/Date	Things I Did	Positive Attributes
Tue 5/7/05	1. Mopped the floors	House Proud
	2. Finished project	Diligent
	3. Played with kids	Fun to be with

Start with noticing three a day if that is comfortable (you can always start with fewer if necessary), but try to build from there, increasing it to 4, or 5 or 6. By doing this, you will not only be acknowledging your positive qualities as things you did in the past, but also acknowledging them as things you are every day.

Positive Qualities Record

To help you make a list of your positive qualities, ask yourself the following questions:

- What do I like about who I am?
- What characteristics do I have that are positive?
- What are some of my achievements?
- What are some challenges I have overcome?
- What are some skills or talents that I have?
- What do others say they like about me?
- What are some attributes I like in others that I also have in common with?
- If someone shared my identical characteristics, what would I admire in them?
- How might someone who cared about me describe me?
- What do I think are bad qualities?
- What bad qualities do I not have?

*Remember to include everything no matter how small, insignificant, modest, or unimportant you think they are

1. _____
2. _____
3. _____
4. _____

5. _____
6. _____
7. _____
8. _____
9. _____
10. _____
11. _____
12. _____
13. _____
14. _____
15. _____
16. _____
17. _____
18. _____
19. _____
20. _____
21. _____
22. _____
23. _____
24. _____
25. _____

Positive You Journal

(Part 1: Past Examples)

For each positive quality that you have written in your Positive Qualities Record, recall specific examples that illustrate that quality. Try to list as examples as you can.

Positive Quality	Specific Example
_____	_____
_____	_____
_____	_____
_____	_____
_____	_____
_____	_____
_____	_____

Positive You Journal

(Part 2: Everyday Examples)

1. For each day of the week, think 3 examples of positive qualities that you have shown during the day
2. Write the day and date, what you had done during the day, and what positive qualities your actions demonstrate

Day/Date	What You Did During the Day	Positive Qualities Shown

Acting Like the Positive You

Another way of promoting a balanced view of yourself is by addressing your behaviors and how you treat yourself. When you think negatively about yourself, how do you tend to behave? Do you treat yourself as someone deserving of fun and recognition for your achievements? Or instead, do you neglect yourself and withdraw from life? If you have problems with low self-esteem, it is likely that you take the latter approach to life. This means that you probably engage in few activities that are pleasurable or do things that are just for you, and discount the things you accomplish from day to day. Taking such an approach keeps all those negative self-evaluations alive.

Experiencing enjoyment and a sense of accomplishment are an important part of everyday experience, which makes us feel good about ourselves and our lives. The problem for people with low self-esteem is that they often believe that they are undeserving. Therefore, enjoyment and achievement does not feature in their day, and this keeps them thinking negatively about who they are as a person. This is something we want to reverse, and get you treating yourself kindly and treating yourself to a fulfilling and satisfying life. Treating yourself well will help you start seeing yourself in a more balanced and accepting light.

Getting Started

The first step to changing the way you treat yourself is to first observe how your life is currently. Using the Weekly Activity

Schedule, start recording the activities you get up to during the week. Then, for each activity, rate the sense of pleasure and achievement (0-10) that you get from doing that activity. When doing this, it is important to remember that a sense of achievement does not only come from doing huge things (e.g., a promotion, an award, graduating), but achievement can come from the day-to-day things (e.g., cooking a nice meal, confronting a situation you had some anxiety about, doing some housework when feeling unmotivated, etc.).
By observing what you do during your week and rating your activities, you can see how much fun or sense of achievement you are having in your average week. If there is not much that is pleasant, fun, or enjoyable to you, this will be a sign that you need to increase your fun activities. By observing how your week is currently, you can also start recognizing your accomplishments and achievements, which you may have ignored or discounted previously, or tackle some tasks to give you a sense of achievement.

Making Changes

Once you have a good sense of what a typical week looks like for you, you can think about what you would like to change. Do you need more fun activities in your week? What activities would be enjoyable, pleasant, or relaxing? What would be something you can do just for you, to treat yourself kindly? On what days or at what times could you do fun things for yourself? Are you avoiding or neglecting things in your life, so that there is little sense of achievement in your week? What could you start doing to rectify this? When could you do these things?

Once you have a sense of what needs changing, it is time to put the changes in place. In this book there is Fun Activities Catalogue. There are 183 activities listed in this catalogue. These are suggestions to help you think about what you might enjoy. You may be able to think of others. Choose two or three from the list to do in the coming week. Remember to also include one or two achievement-type tasks to your schedule as well. Use the worksheet to plan which activity you will do, when you will do it (date), and then rate your sense of pleasure and achievement BEFORE and AFTER the activity. This will let you know if the activity has been helpful. You could also use the Weekly Activity Schedule from before to plan your fun and achievement activities for the week.

Starting Simple

Even though there are many advantages to increasing your fun and achievement, it might not be easy to get started. Often, this is because you have rarely done things just for you, and you think negative thoughts such as "I don't deserve to do things for myself," "It's too hard," "I am not worth it," "I won't enjoy doing this," or "I'll probably fail at this too." These thoughts may stop you from getting started. Often the big mistake people make is trying to do too much too soon.

If you hadn't been doing any running for 6 months, would you try and run a marathon without doing any training? Of course not! You would go on a training program that starts out within your present capabilities, and then slowly build up your fitness and endurance. Similarly, when you are down on yourself, it is unreasonable to expect yourself to be able to jump out of bed and clean the house before going out to meet a friend for a late lunch. If you set your goals too high, you might end up not doing them, become disappointed in yourself, and feel worse than ever about who you are. Instead, plan to do things that are achievable at your current level of functioning. Start with small steps if necessary and slowly build yourself up to the large tasks that seem unmanageable right now. For example, don't try to tidy the whole house in one go – start with one room and just aim to tidy one area. If you're wanting to clean the kitchen, start with the dirty dishes. Then, aim to get the bench tops clean, before you move to the stove. Any task can be broken down into smaller steps until you find something achievable.

Sometimes it is easier to aim to do a task for a set period rather than trying to achieve a set amount. Exercise for 5 to 10 minutes rather than aim to do an hour's worth. Say you will spend 10 minutes weeding the garden rather than aiming to weed a certain area. In this way, it will be easier for you to achieve your goal. In the beginning, the important thing is not what you do or how much you do, but simply the fact that you are DOING. Remember that action is the first step, not motivation, and you will soon find yourself feeling better about doing things for yourself or approaching challenging things.

Weekly Activity Schedule

Use this worksheet to record the activities you get up to during the week. Then, for each activity, rate the sense of pleasure and achievement (1-10) that you get from doing that activity. When you have done this, reflect on what you have recorded. What do you make of your activity schedule.

	Monday	Tuesday	Wednesday	Thursday	Friday	Saturday	Sunday
8-9 am							
9 to 10 am							
10 to 11 am							
11 to 12 pm							
12 to 1 pm							
1 to 2 pm							
2 to 3 pm							
3 to 4 pm							
4 to 5 pm							
5 to 6 pm							
6 to 7 pm							
7 to 8 pm							
8 to 9 pm							
9 to 10 pm							
11 to 12 pm							

Pleasurable Activities Catalogue

The following is a list of activities that might be pleasurable for you. Feel free to add your own pleasurable activities to the list.

1. Soaking in the bathtub
2. Planning my career
3. Collecting things (coins, shells, etc.)
4. Going for a holiday thing
5. Recycling old items
6. Relaxing
7. Going on a date
8. Going to a movie
9. Jogging, walking
10. Listening to music
11. Thinking I have done a full day's work
12. Recalling past parties
13. Buying household gadgets
14. Lying in the sun
15. Planning a career change
16. Laughing
17. Thinking about my past trips
18. Listening to others
19. Reading magazines or newspapers
20. Hobbies (stamp collecting, model building, etc.)
21. Spending an evening with good friends
22. Planning a day's activities
23. Meeting new people
24. Remembering beautiful scenery
25. Saving money
26. Gambling
27. Going to the gym, doing aerobics
28. Eating
29. Thinking how it will be when I finish school
30. Getting out of debt/paying debts
31. Practicing karate, judo, yoga
32. Thinking about retirement
33. Repairing things around the house
34. Working on my car (bicycle)
35. Remembering the words and deeds of loving people
36. Wearing sexy clothes
37. Having quiet evenings
38. Taking care of my plants
39. Buying, selling stocks and shares
79. Making a gift for someone
80. Buying CDs, tapes, records
81. Watching boxing, wrestling
82. Planning parties
83. Cooking, baking
84. Going hiking, bush walking
85. Writing books (poems, articles)
86. Sewing
87. Buying clothes
88. Working
89. Going out to dinner
90. Discussing books
91. Sightseeing
92. Gardening
93. Going to the beauty salon
94. Early morning coffee and newspaper
95. Playing tennis
96. Kissing
97. Watching my children (play)
98. Thinking I have a lot more going for me than most people
99. Going to plays and concerts
100. Daydreaming
101. Planning to go to TAFE or university
102. Going for a drive
103. Listening to a stereo
104. Refinishing furniture
105. Watching videos or DVDs
106. Making lists of tasks
107. Going bike riding
108. Walks on the riverfront/foreshore
109. Buying gifts
110. Travelling to national parks
111. Completing a task
112. Thinking about my achievements
113. Going to a footy game (or rugby, soccer, basketball, etc.)
114. Eating gooey, fattening foods
115. Exchanging emails, chatting on the internet
116. Photography

117. Going fishing
118. Thinking about pleasant events
119. Staying on a diet
120. Star gazing
40. Going swimming
41. Doodling
42. Exercising
43. Collecting old things
44. Going to a party
45. Thinking about buying
46. Playing golf
47. Playing soccer
48. Flying kites
49. Having discussions
50. Having family get-
51. Riding a motorbike
52. Sex
53. Playing squash
54. Going camping
55. Singing around the house
56. Arranging flowers
57. Going to church, praying (practicing religion)
58. Losing weight
59. Going to the beach
60. Thinking I'm an OK person
61. A day with nothing to do
62. Having class reunions
63. Going ice skating, roller skating/blading
64. Going sailing
65. Travelling abroad, interstate or within the state
66. Sketching, painting
67. Doing something spontaneously
68. Doing embroidery, cross stitching
69. Sleeping
70. Driving
71. Entertaining
72. Going to clubs (garden, sewing, etc.)
73. Thinking about getting married
74. Going birdwatching
75. Singing with groups
76. Flirting
77. Playing musical instruments
78. Doing arts and crafts

121. Flying a plane
122. Reading fiction
123. Acting
124. Being alone
125. Writing diary/journal entries or letters
126. Cleaning
127. Reading non-fiction
128. Taking children places
129. Dancing
130. Going on a picnic
131. Thinking "I did that pretty well" after doing something
132. Meditating
133. Playing volleyball
134. Having lunch with a friend
135. Going to the hills
136. Thinking about having a family
137. Thoughts about happy moments in my childhood
138. Splurging
139. Playing cards
140. Having a political discussion
141. Solving riddles mentally
142. Playing cricket
143. Seeing and/or showing photos or slides
144. Knitting/crocheting/quilting
145. Doing crossword puzzles
146. Shooting pool/Playing billiards
147. Dressing up and looking nice
148. Reflecting on how I've improved
149. Buying things for myself
150. Talking on the phone
151. Going to museums, art galleries 152. Thinking religious thoughts
153. Surfing the internet
154. Lighting candles
155. Listening to the radio
156. Going crabbing or prawning
157. Having coffee at a cafe
158. Getting/giving a massage
159. Saying "I love you"
160. Thinking about my good qualities
161. Buying books
162. Having a spa, or sauna
163. Going skiing

164. Going canoeing or white-water rafting
165. Going bowling
166. Doing woodworking
167. Fantasizing about the future
168. Doing ballet, jazz/tap dancing
169. Debating
170. Playing computer games
171. Having an aquarium
172. Erotica (sex books, movies)
173. Going horseback riding
174. Going rock climbing
175. Thinking about becoming active in the community
176. Doing something new
177. Making jigsaw puzzles
178. Thinking I'm a person who can cope
179. Playing with my pets
180. Having a barbecue
181. Rearranging the furniture in my house
182. Buying new furniture
183. Going window shopping

Other Ideas:
_____
_____
_____
_____
_____
_____
_____
_____
_____
_____
_____
_____
_____
_____
_____
_____

Adjusting Rules & Assumptions
Introduction

In previous sections, we discussed biased expectations and negative self-evaluations and introduced some strategies for you to work at challenging them. In the previous section, we discussed the importance of accepting yourself and explored strategies for identifying and acknowledging your positive qualities and experiences. We hope that you have found these strategies helpful in improving how you feel about, and see, yourself. Now that you have had some experience in working through these strategies, it is also important that we tackle some of the more difficult issues and work toward addressing negative core beliefs. In this section, we will discuss adjusting and changing the unhelpful rules and assumptions that restrict your behavior and keep your negative core beliefs alive.

Rules for Living

Here are some things to review and keep in mind, before we begin tackling our unhelpful rules.

Rules are learned. It is not often that unhelpful rules are formally taught. Rather these are developed through trial and error and observations you had made in your earlier life experiences. You may not consciously know that you have developed these rules, but they consistently influence how you behave and live your life anyway. These rules often grew out of the conclusions you made about yourself because of your earlier life experiences. Therefore, these rules are also unique to you.

Rules can be culture-specific. The rules and assumptions for living that you have developed reflect the norms and culture of the family and the society or community in which you grew up. For example, you might have grown up in a family where boys are favored over girls and if you are female, you might have concluded that you are a second-class citizen. You might then have learned the rule, "Women must always be subservient to men," and continue to live according to this rule even if circumstances are different now.

Rules can be stubborn and resist change. Rules for living not only guide your behavior, they also influence how you perceive, interpret, and absorb information throughout your life. We talked about how there are many things happening, and there is a lot of information available, around us. Often, we are not aware of all that is going on because our brains would be bombarded with too much information if we tried to make sense of everything. Therefore, we are equipped with an ability to sift out information and focus on only those things that are important to us. Unfortunately, this could also work against us because we tend to only pay attention to, and make sense of, those things that are consistent with our beliefs and rules. So, if you have the negative core belief, "I am an unattractive person," and the rule "I must always be funny and witty or else no one will like me," you might only notice the person who doesn't laugh at your remarks and not the other three who were laughing heartily. You might also then interpret that as "People didn't laugh at my jokes, so they must not like me." Therefore, unhelpful rules for living and negative core beliefs can be resistant to change. However, now that you know this, you can learn to notice other things as well and to challenge any unhelpful interpretations so that you can have a more balanced view of yourself.

Rules for Living: What's Helpful, What's Not

Rules and assumptions for living guide our behavior and enable us to cope with our everyday lives. Rules for living are necessary for us to make sense of the world around us and to help us function on a day to-day basis. So, having rules is helpful. The question is what type of rules do we have? There are many rules for living that are helpful.

Helpful rules are realistic, flexible, and adaptable, and they enable us to function healthily and safely. For example, "People should not drive when they have had too much to drink (i.e., have a blood alcohol level of more than .05)" is a helpful rule. These types of rules are realistic, that is, there is evidence to support them. There is evidence that the judgement of people who have more than a blood alcohol level of .05 can become impaired. They are less able to see clearly and concentrate on what they are doing. So, based on this evidence, keeping this rule can help ensure our survival! Helpful rules are also those that are flexible and adaptable. This means that they allow you to adapt your behavior to various situations. No one can be certain about everything in life nor does one have control over everything. That is why rules that have some

'give' in them are probably more helpful than those that are absolutistic. Consider the rule, "It would be great if we could all try our best and work as hard as we can for this project" compared with "We must always be the best at everything we do, at all costs." In the first rule, we are asked to work to the best of our abilities, given the circumstances, for a project. This means that the rule takes into consideration the times that for some reason, we are not able to match the standards that we reached previously. Perhaps we are ill or are experiencing a problematic situation in our personal lives. The rule is also flexible in that it applies to a situation (a project) as there are other times when we may choose not to work so hard at something (ex, gardening, cooking, or cleaning our house). We may decide that we want to work but also to take it a little easier.

Unhelpful rules are unrealistic, unreasonable, excessive, rigid, and unadaptable. Look at the second rule in the above paragraph. According to that rule, we have to achieve a particular standard ("best at everything") in every situation ("always") and not caring about what we might have to do or give up achieving it ("at all costs"). If we believed strongly in this rule and made ourselves live up to it every day, what would happen? We will probably feel strong negative emotions when the rule is broken, which is quite likely. The reality is that we cannot be the best all the time. There are times when others might achieve better results. This rule also ensures that our self-esteem remains low because it is setting us up to fail.
Let's explore further how unhelpful rules keep low self-esteem going.

Unhelpful Rules & Low Self-Esteem

Low self-esteem is viewing yourself and valuing your self-worth in a negative way. This is reflected in the negative core beliefs you might have about yourself, such as, "I am unlovable," or "I am not important." As discussed in, you might have come to these conclusions because of significant negative experiences early in life. To help you get by and manage from day to day, you might have developed rules and assumptions to help protect your self-esteem.

Unfortunately, these rules and assumptions are usually unrealistic, unreasonable, rigid, and unadaptable. Let's say, for example, that you have the belief, "I am incompetent." You might have developed the rule and assumption "I must never ask for help, because if I do, people will laugh at me" or "I must never take on a task that seems too difficult for me because if I don't do well, people will think I'm a total idiot." If you can stick to, and carry out, these rules and assumptions, you might feel okay about yourself because then no one will know how bad you are at doing things. But what is the effect of having such rules?

Although these rules appear to help protect your self-esteem, they keep your negative core beliefs and your low self-esteem in place – they are 'locked in' as it were. Living up to such rules and assumptions means that your behavior is restricted in such a way that these rules and your negative core beliefs do not have the opportunity to be challenged. Let's continue with the previous example, with the rule and assumption, "I must never ask for help, because if I do, people will laugh at me." If you never ask for help, you will not be able to check out what people's responses are if you do. If you occasionally asked for help, you might find that some people were quite happy to lend a helping hand and did not laugh at you. In this way, your assumption that people would laugh at you if you asked for help would have been challenged. However, because of your reluctance in asking for help, you don't get a chance to debunk it. As such, your rule and assumption stay in place and your negative core belief also remains intact. Not only do such unhelpful rules and assumptions keep low self-esteem in place, they also put a considerable amount of pressure on you. Note that the rule is "I must never ask for help." The words "must" and "never" are an indication of the inflexibility of the rule. The rule demands that you behave in a way all the time. It does not allow you to behave differently in, or adapt to, different environments and situations.

Identifying My Unhelpful Rules & Assumptions

Let's now begin to identify what unhelpful rules and assumptions you might have developed for yourself to live by. You might already have an idea of these now that you have learned to challenge your biased expectations and negative self-evaluations. When identifying your rules and assumptions, ask yourself:

- What do I expect of myself when I am at work or school?
- What standards do I expect myself to meet?
- What would I accept and not accept?
- What do I expect of myself when I am socializing?
- What do I expect of myself in my various roles – child, friend, partner, parent, staff member/supervisor?
- What do I expect of myself regarding leisure or fun activities, and self-care?

Rules and assumptions for living can be in the form of statements such as:

"I must/should have to always…or else…."	Ex, "I must always be the best at everything." "I have to always keep it together and control my emotions."
"I must/should never…"	Ex, "I must never show any sign of weakness or back away from a challenge," "I should never ask for something that I need."
"If…, then…,"	Ex, "If I let people know the real me, they will think I'm a total loser."

The following are other sources from which you might be able to identify your rules and assumptions for living.

Thought Diaries. What you have recorded in your Thought Diaries are biased expectations and negative self-evaluations, which are also known as unhelpful thoughts. Often, there is another layer behind those unhelpful thoughts. For example, thoughts such as, "This report really sucks. I didn't have time to include colored charts. I should have done better," might reflect the rule, "I have to do everything perfectly." Usually, there are rules and assumptions for living that are already present that generate or "drive" the unhelpful thoughts. Can you recognize if there are any rules for living reflected in your unhelpful thoughts?

Themes. Another way of identifying the rules and assumptions that guide your behavior is to ask yourself if you notice any themes that might be common to the concerns you have or the issues that you are preoccupied with. You could ask yourself questions such as:

- In what types of situations might I experience the most anxiety or self-doubt?
- What aspects of myself am I most hard on?
- What types of negative predictions do I make?
- What behaviors in other people are linked with me feeling less confident about myself?

Negative Evaluations of Self & Others. Ask yourself:

- In what types of situations do I put myself down?
- What aspects of myself do I criticize most?
- What does this say about what I expect of myself?
- What might happen if I relax my standards?
- What type of person do I think I might become?
- What don't I allow myself to do?
- What do I criticize in other people?
- What expectations of them do I have?
- What standards do I expect them to live up to?

Direct Messages/Family Sayings. Sometimes, your rules and assumptions for living might be direct messages given to you when you were a child or adolescent. Ask yourself:

- What was I told about what I should and should not do?
- What happened when I did not obey those rules?
- What was I told then?
- For what was I punished, criticized, and ridiculed?
- What was said to me when I was not able to meet expectations?
- How did people who were important to me respond when I was naughty, made mistakes, or didn't do well at school?
- What did I have to do to receive praise, affection, or warmth?

Some of those messages you received when you were much younger could be in the form of sayings that some families might have, or some sort of a "motto." For example, adults in families might say, "The only person you can depend on is yourself," "People who are nice to you always want something in return," "Practice makes perfect," "If you can't do something well, you might as well not try," or "If you don't aim high, you will never be successful." Did your family have any sayings or mottos that you remember or use today?

Now that you have read this section on identifying your rules and assumptions for living, have you been able to identify or recognize any that are operating right now in your life? What are some of those rules and assumptions? Take a few minutes to write them down.

Adjusting the Rules

By now, you might have come to recognize some unhelpful rules and assumptions for living that you might have developed when you were younger and have been trying to live according to them. Just as in the previous Sections, you can work at challenging your rules and assumptions for living in a step-by-step way using a worksheet. If you have worked through the previous Sections, you will probably find that changing the rules is not that difficult. It isn't easy, but it might not be that difficult either, given that you have already had some practice at challenging your biased expectations and negative self-evaluations. You will find a worksheet for you to work through. Before doing that, read the following notes that will provide a guide for you.

1. Identify an unhelpful rule and/or assumption that you would like to challenge. If you have many rules and assumptions and are not sure which one to work on first, choose one that is related to an aspect of your life that you really want to change (e.g., your social life or your relationship with your colleagues).

2. Have a think about how this rule and/or assumption for living has impacted your life. Ask yourself: What aspect of my life has this rule had an impact? Has it affected my relationships, work, or studies, how I take care of myself or engage in social or leisure activities? How do I respond when things don't go well? How do I respond to challenging situations or new opportunities? How do I express my emotions? Am I able to ask for my needs to be met? Evaluating the effect of unhelpful rules and assumptions on your life is important because you not only want to change and adjust these rules, you also want to change how they affect your life.

3. Ask yourself, how do you know when this rule is in operation? How do you know when the rule is active in your life? How do you feel? What are the things you do and say (to yourself or others)?

4. Ask yourself, "Where did the rule come from?" The purpose of this question is to provide a context for your rule and assumption. It is to help you understand how this rule developed and what might have kept it going all this while. As we have discussed before, unhelpful rules and assumptions might have made sense at the time when you were experiencing a difficult situation and you adopted them so that you could cope and function from day to day. However, the main issue is whether this rule or assumption is still relevant today. Ask yourself, "Is this rule still necessary today? Is it useful?"

5. Next, ask yourself, "In what ways is this rule (and/or assumption) unreasonable?" Remember that we have discussed that unhelpful rules and assumptions are inflexible and rigid. Sometimes when you live according to such rules and assumptions, you don't recognize that the world around us does not behave that way in general. Also, these rules and assumptions were made when you were a child or young person. As an adult now, you don't have to live according to the rules you made as a child.

6. Although unhelpful rules and assumptions are not beneficial in the long term, there might be certain advantages in living according to these rules. It is probably why these rules and assumptions are still intact. Make a list of these advantages. Ask yourself, "What advantages do I gain from living according to this rule and/or assumption? What benefits have I obtained? How have these been helpful? What do they protect me from?"

7. What are the disadvantages of living according to this rule and assumption? You have identified the advantages, but it is also important to evaluate whether or not the advantages are really genuine. Then ask yourself about how this rule/assumption might limit your opportunities, prevent you from experiencing fun and pleasure, downplay your achievements and successes, negatively impact on your relationships, or prevent you from achieving your life goals. Write these down on the worksheet and then compare them with the advantages you had written down. Do the disadvantages outweigh the advantages? If it is the other way around, then maybe you need not challenge this rule and assumption. If you decide that this rule and assumption is not helpful, then let's move on to the next important point.

8. Now, think carefully about what might be a more balanced rule – what would be more realistic, flexible, and helpful? Try and think about how you could maximize the advantages and minimize the disadvantages of the old rule. Think about the ability to adapt this rule to different situations. Consider using less extreme terms such as "sometimes," "some people," "prefer," "would like," "it would be nice if," compared with "must," "should," "it would be terrible if…" For example, instead of the unhelpful rule, "I must do whatever it takes to stay slim, or else I will never have any friends," consider the alternative "I will try to maintain a healthy lifestyle and it would be nice if I could continue to be slim. However, it is unlikely that my friends only like me because I am slim." Balanced rules and assumptions might end up being longer than old ones. This is because they are more 'sophisticated' – you are making it more realistic, flexible, and adaptable. If you find it difficult to think of an alternative rule and/or assumption that is more balanced, don't worry. Just give it a try and put it in practice for a week or two. You can always revise your rule and adjust it as you become more familiar with the process of challenging and adjusting your unhelpful rules and assumptions.

9. The final step is to consider what you could do to put your new rule and assumption into practice. Why do you think it might be important to do this? Remember that your old rule and assumption had been in operation for some time now, so it is important that you not only have a new rule but new behaviors so that the new rule can be 'house-broken' and settle into your balanced belief system.

This is an "Adjusting the Rules" worksheet, try working through a worksheet yourself.

Adjusting the Rules

Rule and/or assumption I would like to adjust
What impact has this rule or assumption had on my life
How do I Know this rule is in operation?
Where did this rule or assumption come from?
In what ways is this rule or assumption unreasonable?
Advantages of this Rule **Disadvantage of this Rule**
What is an alternative rule or assumption that is more balanced and flexible?
What can I do to put this rule or assumption into practice daily?

Following Through

Now that you have worked through the worksheet, it might be a good idea to write down your new rule on a card that you can carry around with you and review every now and again. You could also write down the things you will aim to do to put this rule in practice.

Importantly, put the new rule into practice by carrying out those actions that you have planned. Although it might seem difficult to you now, it will get easier as you keep doing them. These behaviors are new to you so it's normal that they don't seem to be done naturally. With practice, will come progress!

Sometimes, the old rule might be activated again, so be prepared. This is because the old rule has been with you for a while and you have become quite used to it. But remember, circumstances have changed, and the old rule is outdated. This is when challenging the old rule is important, as well as reviewing your flashcard, and practicing the new behaviors.

Developing Balanced Core Beliefs
Introduction

We have now come to the final step in tackling low self-esteem – changing the negative core beliefs you have about yourself. In earlier Sections, you learned how to tackle the negative unhelpful thoughts you might have in day-to-day situations, which sprout from your negative core beliefs. Earlier, you learned how to change the unhelpful rules and assumptions that have kept your negative core beliefs intact. These previous Sections have put you in a strong position to tackle the negative core beliefs now directly that are at the root of your low self-esteem. All the hard work you have done so far has been undermining your negative core beliefs, shaking the ground beneath them, and sowing the seed of doubt as to how accurate they are. So, let's finish the job, and focus on adjusting those negative core beliefs – from negative and biased, to balanced and realistic.

Identifying Your Negative Core Belief

Remember, your negative core beliefs reflect the negative, broad, and generalized judgements you have made about yourself, based on some negative experiences you might have had during your earlier years. Based on the work you have done in the earlier Sections, you may already know what those beliefs are, and you may have begun to question them. However, let's really focus on this now.

If you are not clear as to what your negative core beliefs are yet, you need to first pin them down and identify them, before you can start changing them. Reflecting on the work you have already done will provide information and clues as to what your negative core beliefs are. To uncover those negative core beliefs, you will need to think about the implications of the specific clues and information you already have, that is, think about what they say about the overall view you have of yourself. Important questions to ask yourself throughout this 'identification' process is: What does this information mean about me as a person? What does this clue say about who I am? Asking yourself these questions will help you uncover your negative core beliefs from specific thoughts and experiences you have already identified.

Below are the various clues and information you can use to identify your negative core beliefs. Go through each of them, and see if you can discover the specific negative core beliefs that ring true for you.

Negative Life Experiences

The negative life experiences that you identified as contributing to the development of your low self-esteem could provide clues as to what your negative core beliefs are. Reflect on these experiences and ask yourself the following questions. Jot down any ideas about the negative core beliefs that come to mind.

Did these experiences lead me to think there was something wrong with me in some way? If so, what was wrong?

_____

_____

_____

_____

Do I remember specific situations that accompany the negative thoughts or feelings I have about myself? What do my memories of these situations say about me as a person?

_____

_____

_____

_____

Can I link a specific person I know to the way I feel about myself? Has that person used certain words to describe me? What does their treatment of me say about me as a person?

_____

_____

_____

_____

Biased Expectations

The biased expectations that you identified could provide some ideas as to what your negative core beliefs are. Reflect on the key concerns you identified in your Thought Diaries for biased expectations, and ask yourself the following questions. Jot down any ideas about the negative core beliefs that come to mind.

If my biased expectations were to come true, what would that mean about me as a person?

_____

_____

_____

_____

If I didn't avoid or escape or use my safety behaviors, what would I be worried about revealing to other people about who I am?

_____

_____

_____

_____

Negative Self-Evaluations

The negative self-evaluations you uncovered will also provide clues regarding your negative core beliefs. Think about the sorts of criticisms you made of yourself in your Thought Diaries for negative self-evaluations, and ask yourself the following questions. Jot down any ideas about the negative core beliefs that come to mind.

What do my negative self-evaluations say about me as a person?

_____

_____

_____

_____

What are the common themes, labels, words, or names I use to describe myself? What do they mean about me?

_____

_____

_____

_____

Do my negative self-evaluations remind me of criticisms I have received from others when I was young? What do those criticisms tell me about myself?

_____

_____

_____

_____

What things make me critical of myself? What do these things say about who I am?

_____

_____

_____

_____

Difficulties Promoting Balanced Self-Evaluations

The difficulties you may have had with focusing on the positive you (by writing down your positive qualities) and acting like the positive you (by doing pleasant activities that are just for yourself) may give you some ideas regarding your negative core beliefs. Reflect on any troubles you had with thinking about yourself kindly and treating yourself kindly, and ask yourself the following questions. Jot down any ideas about the negative core beliefs that come to mind.

What made it difficult to think about myself kindly or treat myself kindly?

___

What was I telling myself when I tried to do these things?

___

What do my reactions to thinking/treating myself well tell me about how I see myself?

___

<u>Perceived Outcomes of Not Fulfilling the Rules</u>

In a prior section, you clearly identified your unhelpful rules and assumptions. You can also use these to uncover your negative core beliefs. Think about what you fear will happen if your rules are broken. Sometimes your rule will incorporate the negative core belief (ex., "If I don't do things perfectly, I am incompetent," "If people see the real me, then they will know I am inferior," "If I disappoint someone, then I am a bad person."). Ask yourself the following question and jot down any ideas about the negative core beliefs that come to mind.

If my rule was broken, then what would that mean about me?

___

Using all the above clues and asking yourself what these things tell you about how you see yourself will help you to uncover your negative core beliefs. Once you think you have a clear idea as to what they are, write them down in the space below.

_____

_____

_____

_____

_____

_____

_____

_____

_____

Adjusting Your Negative Core Beliefs

1. Choose One Negative Core Belief

    If you have identified many negative core beliefs, choose only ONE to begin working on. You could choose the one that is of greatest concern to work on now or one that is related to any biased expectations, negative self-evaluations, or unhelpful rules and assumptions that you have previously worked on. Write that negative core belief in the top box of the 'Adjusting Core Beliefs Worksheet'. Also note how much you believe the negative core belief at now, when it's most convincing, and when it's least convincing. Note how the negative core belief makes you feel. Throughout this Section, you will need to keep referring to this worksheet and completing the relevant sections as we go. This will ensure that as you work through your negative core belief and tackle it, you have a clear record of this process to refer to at any time in the future.

    Once you have worked through the process of adjusting this first negative core belief, you will then be able to apply it to other negative core beliefs you might want to change.

2. Develop a Balanced Core Belief

    Now it's time to develop an alternative core belief to replace your old negative one.

When developing a new core belief, you want to aim for something that is more positive, balanced, and realistic. Think of something that is a more accurate reflection of yourself. It is important that the work you do on your negative core beliefs is not just about squashing the belief that you have been carrying around, but also about promoting a new balanced view of yourself. So, it is not so much about saying what you are not (ex., "I am not stupid"), but more about saying what you are (ex., "I am capable in many ways").

From the work you have done in previous Sections, you may already have some idea of what a more balanced core belief might be. It might be the opposite of your old belief (ex., "I am incompetent" ¤ "I am competent"), a more moderate view of yourself (ex., "I am a failure" ¤ "I am great at many things, average at other things, and weaker in some areas like anyone else"), or something else (ex., "I am no good" ¤ "I am a worthwhile person"). The important thing is that the new belief is more balanced, weighing up all the information (not just the negative) available, and including both your strengths and weaknesses. When developing a new core belief, ensure that your worth as a person is not being determined by only your faults or weaknesses. Also make sure that you are not painting an overly positive view of yourself (ex., "I am perfect in every way"), as this will be unrealistic, and it is unlikely that you will believe it. Remember not to discount any new alternative core beliefs on the basis that you don't fulfil these 100% (ex., "I can't put down that I am competent because sometimes I get things wrong."). No one is capable of such feats of perfection, so instead, accept that you are your new view of yourself – not perfect, but "good enough."

Now that you have an idea of your new balanced core belief, write it in the 'Adjusting Negative Core Beliefs' worksheet'. Also note how much you believe this new core belief at various times (now, when it is most convincing, and when it is least convincing) and how it makes you feel when you reflect on it. In these early stages, you might not believe it a whole lot. That is to be expected, given that you have carried the other negative view of yourself around with you for some time. To help you be more open to the new balanced view of yourself, let's work through the process further.

3. Examining the Evidence for Old Beliefs

To start to chip away at your old negative core belief, we first need to examine the evidence you base this belief on. What evidence do you have for this negative view of yourself? What experiences do you use to justify this negative core belief? To try to uncover what you base your belief on, ask yourself the following questions:

- Are there current problems I am having that I base this belief on? (ex., problems with depression or anxiety, relationship problems, etc.)
- Am I condemning myself because I need help and can't manage alone? (ex., turning to friends, family, or mental health professionals for assistance)
- Am I condemning myself based on past mistakes I have made? (ex., failing school, trouble with the law, infidelity in past relationships, etc.)
- Am I condemning myself based on specific weaknesses of mine? (ex., not being academically minded, not being good at sport, etc.)

- Am I condemning myself based on my physical characteristics or my personality attributes? (ex., my body size, my attractiveness or my shyness, my untidiness)
- Do I base my view of myself on how I compare to other people? (ex., whether I am better than them in certain tasks, achievements, appearance, etc.)
- Do I use how other people treat or have treated me as a basis for how I view myself? (ex., abuse, neglect, mistreatment)
- Do I use the behavior of other people as a basis for how I view myself? (ex., my child's poor behavior)
- Have I lost something that is important to my self-worth? (ex., job loss, relationship break-up)

Once you have a clear idea of some of the evidence you use to justify the negative view you have of yourself, write the evidence down in the column marked "Evidence For" your Old Negative Core Belief, on the worksheet. When you have identified the evidence for your negative core belief, it is time to assess how credible and accurate the evidence is. This is like being a lawyer who questions how good or trustworthy the evidence is, whether or not it stands up under scrutiny. This is where you also ask yourself: Are there alternative ways of understanding this evidence? Are there other explanations you have not considered? Are there other ways of interpreting or making sense of the evidence, other than condemning who you are as a person? Try to uncover other ways of understanding the evidence by asking yourself the following questions:

- Are there other explanations for the current problems I am having, other than personal shortcomings? (ex., "I have not been meeting my commitments – not because I am lazy – but because procrastination and neglect are symptoms of depression")
- Are there benefits in getting help from other people? How do I view people that ask me for help? (ex., "I guess two heads are better than one, and I don't think badly of people who ask me for help, sometimes it takes a stronger person to admit they need help")
- Is it reasonable to base my self-esteem on my past mistakes? (ex., "Everyone makes mistakes. It is unfair to beat myself up over things I can't change")
- Is it reasonable to base my self-esteem on my specific weaknesses? (ex., "Just because I am not good at something, does not make me useless as a whole person. Everyone has their strengths and weaknesses")
- Is it reasonable to base my self-esteem on my appearance or on certain personality attributes I have? (ex., "I don't' judge others by how they look, so why do it to myself"; "Just because I am shy, doesn't mean I am a freak, it is just who I am, everyone is different in that way")
- Is it fair to compare myself to others, and base my self-esteem on whether I am better than they are? (ex., "Just because someone is better than me at this doesn't make them a better person. There will always be people I am better than at certain things and others who are better than me at certain things")
- What are other reasons for the way people treat or have treated me, other than personal shortcomings? (ex., "The way they treated me was probably due to the type of person they are and problems they have, rather than who I am")

- Can I be 100% responsible for another person's behavior? (ex., "As much as I try to do my best, I don't have absolute control over my child's behavior. There are other factors involved, it is not all my fault")

Once you have identified some other ways of understanding the evidence for your old negative core belief, list these new perspectives in the column marked "Alternatives Ways of Looking at the Evidence" on the worksheet. Now that you have completed this section of the worksheet, what did you make of what you had written? Hopefully this exercise will show you that the evidence you base the old negative view of yourself on is not totally accurate and probably unfair in many ways. Did you find this difficult to do? It can be in the beginning, because you have always accepted your negative core beliefs and the evidence for them. However, with practice, and putting on a different perspective (like putting on a different pair of spectacles), you'll soon find that you can do this exercise with ease.

4. Supporting New Beliefs

You have spent time gaining a new perspective on the evidence you have used in the past to support your old negative view of yourself. Now let's turn to supporting the new balanced view of yourself that you have developed. To support your new core beliefs, to take them on board, let them sink in, and make them believable, you need to do two things. Firstly, you need to gather evidence that is consistent with this new view of yourself, paying attention to evidence from the past/present and looking out for appropriate evidence in the future. Secondly, you need to act on, and experiment with, this new view of yourself. This means that you need to test it out, try it on for size, and act in ways that are consistent with the new you.

Evidence

In previous sections, we have discussed how when you have a core belief about yourself, you will tend to only pay attention to things that confirm your belief. Therefore, to enhance the new balanced view of yourself, you will need to start paying attention to evidence from the past and present that confirms this new view. You also need to be ready to pay attention to evidence that arises in the future that confirms this new view. On the 'Adjusting Negative Core Beliefs' worksheet, fill in past or present examples or experiences you have had that are consistent with your new balanced core belief. When doing this, pay attention to things that have happened that support this kinder view of yourself. Once you have done this, fill in the types of evidence likely to arise in the future, which will confirm your new balanced view. This will act as a reminder of what to be on the lookout for, to help you strengthen this kinder view of yourself.

Experiments

The last part of adjusting your negative core beliefs involves behaving as if the new balanced view of yourself is true. Now it doesn't sound very good, does it? But of course, it is true! It's just that you might not quite believe it yet. Do you agree? This is because you have been carrying around the negative core beliefs for a while. However, you are beginning to loosen their hold on you. Let's loosen it further by changing how you behave and live your life! Ask yourself how someone who believed this kinder view of themselves might act or behave from day to day? How you can test out this new perspective you have of yourself? What things could you do to obtain more evidence for your new balanced core belief? What new experiences might further support this new perspective you are developing?

In general, to create new opportunities for more experiences that will support your new core belief will involve:

- Approaching rather than avoiding things
- Sticking with challenges rather than escaping
- Stopping safety behaviors and approaching things without taking precautions
- Treating yourself well
- Doing pleasant things for yourself
- Taking note of achievements and positive qualities
- Being active and engaged in life
- Being assertive

At a more specific level, think about exactly what you could do to 'test-drive' this new view of yourself. Exactly what new behaviors will you need to try out? How will you be behaving differently to before? Once you have some specific ideas about how to experiment with this new core belief, write these down in the "New Behavior/Experiments" section of the 'Adjusting Negative Core Beliefs' worksheet.

5. Evaluating Your Beliefs

   Now that you have been through the step-by-step process for adjusting your negative core beliefs, it is important to reflect on what impact this process has had on you. You can do this by re-rating how much you now believe your old negative core belief and compare it to how much you now believe your new balanced core belief. Complete these ratings at the bottom of the worksheet.

<u>An Ongoing Process</u>

It is important to remember that changing your core belief about yourself is a difficult task that might take some time and practice. It will involve revisiting the steps in this Section many times, reflecting on what you have written, and perhaps adding more things. It will involve continually re-training your attention in everyday life so that you take note of all the future evidence that will arise to further support your new belief. It will involve behaving differently and using experiments to help accumulate more experiences and evidence for your new belief. It is an ongoing process. Remember, you have carried this old belief around for many years, so it will take some time to adjust it and embrace your new belief. However, you will find that if you continue to apply these strategies over time, your conviction in your old negative core beliefs will decrease and your conviction in your new balanced core beliefs will rise.

Healthy Self-Esteem
Introduction

Congratulations on making it to the end of this section! We're glad you stayed on with us. If you haven't read all the Sections, it might be good to go back to the ones you missed. In this Section, you will find a summary of all the important concepts and strategies introduced to you in the previous Sections and a discussion on how to continue to improve on what you have learned and maintain your gains.

Putting It All Together

Just as we provided a model to help you understand how low self-esteem developed and what kept it going, we will leave you with a model of healthy self-esteem. This model brings all the important concepts and strategies you have learned together.

This model begins with an at-risk situation and the activation of old negative core beliefs. Having healthy self-esteem doesn't mean that you will never encounter an at-risk situation again. It also doesn't mean that you will never again think of yourself in a negative light. Everyone might think of themselves in a negative way or get down on themselves at times. The important thing to remember is not to do it too often. Healthy self-esteem is about thinking about ourselves and our worth in a BALANCED way. It is okay and appropriate that we recognize our weaknesses. What we need to do is accept that we all have weaknesses, and decide about whether we want to improve on them. We also need to recognize, acknowledge, and celebrate our strengths and successes. Also, don't forget any skills and abilities that might be neutral. Remember, it's all about being balanced!

The reason we might still encounter at-risk situations is that we cannot change our past experiences. We discussed that some of these experiences, especially if they are negative, can influence how we see ourselves and the rules and assumptions that we have developed. So, it is because we cannot go back and change those experiences that they might have a lingering effect on our self-esteem. The important thing to remember is that the effect of your past experiences on how you see yourself can be worn down the more you practice those strategies in the previous Sections.

So, the model of healthy self-esteem begins with an at-risk situation and the activation of old negative core beliefs. However, by this time, you will be able to tackle any biased expectations or negative self-evaluations by using Thought Diaries to challenge them. You will also have learned to identify and celebrate your positive qualities and recognize new achievements. It is also important that you engage in helpful behaviors, which means that you are dropping any avoidance, escaping, use of safety measures, approaching new situations with an open mind, engaging in life and doing pleasant activities, treating yourself kindly, and not withdrawing. If you then add to these, the adjusting of your old negative core beliefs and unhelpful rules and assumptions, and put these new rules and assumptions into practice…the possible consequences of all these actions are numerous! You might encounter opportunities for new experiences and new learning. Unhelpful rules and assumptions, and old negative core beliefs may or may not be confirmed, but there are possibilities for adjustments being made and increased flexibility in the way you see things. Finally, your threshold for at-risk situations might be increased. This means that you are not as sensitive to possible negative situations and will be more open-minded and balanced in how you view new situations.

Model of Healthy Self-Esteem

At-Risk Situation

Situation in which unhelpful rules & assumptions
Are under threat of being broken or are broken

⇩

Activation of Old Negative Core Beliefs

Develop Realistic Expectations   **Develop Balanced Self-Evaluation**

Use Thought Diaries   Use Thought Diaries

Engage in Helpful Behavior

- Approach challenges with open mind
- Stop avoidance, escaping & safety behaviors
- Treat yourself well
- Engage in life
- No withdrawal or isolation

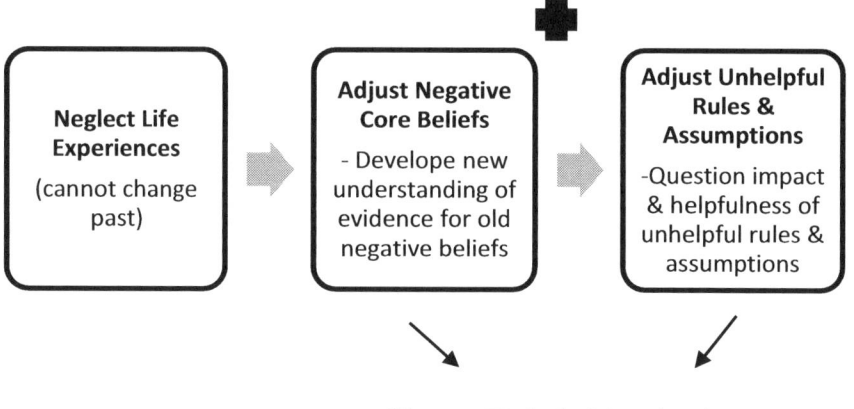

Change Unhelpful Behavior
- **Put new rules into practice**

Possible Consequence
- **Opportunities for new experiences**

Keep Practicing

Now that you have come to the end of this information package, the most important thing for you now is to keep practicing the strategies you have learned in all the Sections. This means continuing to apply all the useful skills and insights about yourself you might have gained. If you continue practicing the concepts and skills you have learned, they will become healthy habits that have been integrated into your lifestyle.

There are a few things to keep in mind now that you have learned some important skills in overcoming low self-esteem. One area to think about is how to maintain the gains that you have made. Another area to think about is how to minimize setbacks that might occur.

Maintaining Gains

It is important to recognize the progress that you've made, and as your self-esteem improves, it is helpful and appropriate to pat yourself on the back and celebrate your achievements. This will encourage you to keep going – to keep practicing and applying the new skills you have learned. Maintaining the gains, you have made relies on you continuing to practice these skills. Remember, developing new skills to challenge what may be years' worth of old habits takes time and persistence.

So, there are some important things you will need to do to make the most of what you have learned to stay well or gain that extra improvement. The easiest way to summarize this is by looking at the "Healthy Self-Esteem" worksheet. It shows the main strategies you have learned to tackle low self-esteem and develop a more balanced view of yourself. Continuing to work on these strategies will help you continue maintaining your gains.

You will notice that on the "Healthy Self-Esteem" worksheet, there are some key things that you have learned over this series of Sections to manage low self-esteem:

- You have learned how to adjust your core beliefs and rules, so that they are more reasonable, flexible, balanced, and realistic
- You have learned to question and test out negative thoughts (ex, biased expectations, and negative self-evaluations) and address unhelpful behaviors in day-to-day situations
- You have learned to promote and support balanced self-evaluations by paying attention to your positive qualities and treating yourself well from day to day.

Minimizing Setbacks

Setbacks or slip-ups in progress can happen at any time and are to be expected. Try not to fall into the trap of believing that you are 'back to square one' as this will only make you feel worse. Change is not a steady process, it's more like the old saying: "Two steps forward, one step back" from time to time.

Think about how you learned to ride a bike. It probably took a few unsteady attempts and a few falls before you gained your balance. Even when you get your balance, you might still be unsteady when travelling over new ground, or on different surfaces. In the same way, different situations or times in your life may be more challenging, and may require extra effort and persistence (i.e., more challenging of biased expectations or negative self-evaluations, more pleasant activities, more paying attention to positive qualities, more experimenting with your behaviors, etc.). Even after much practice, there may be times when you think you've slipped back and feel a little off balance. Developing new skills is never a smooth process, you're always being faced with new challenges and different situations to apply those skills.

There are several reasons for setbacks occurring. There may be an increase in physical or mental stress. Just like riding a bike over challenging terrain, physical and mental stress can be challenges to the new ways of thinking and behaving that you have developed, and you may go back to old habits. Also, when we are physically unwell, we are less likely to have the mental or physical energy required to challenge or experiment with our negative thoughts, rule or beliefs, to treat ourselves well, or think of our positive qualities.

It may help to remind yourself that most people have 'down days' or days where life's hassles are harder to deal with – it's part of being human! Use the Thought Diary skills you have learned to help when these situations occur. Also, you can use setbacks as a way of learning something new about yourself to help avoid similar problems in the future.

Preventing Major Setbacks

As you are progressing, try not to focus too much on small setbacks. If you are experiencing several small setbacks, then there are some ways of preventing a major setback.

1. Identify Early Warning Signs

    The first step is to look out for your own early warning signs. Some common examples are:
    - Spending increased time expecting the worst or being self-critical
    - Reverting to unhelpful behaviors (e.g., avoidance, escape, safety behaviors, withdrawal, isolation, neglect, passivity, etc.)
    - An increase in anxiety or depression.

2. Revise Skills

    Think about the skills you have learned and what has been helpful in addressing your low-self-esteem (ex., challenging/experimenting with biased expectations and negative self-evaluations, paying attention to positive qualities, engaging in fun and achievement activities, treating yourself kindly, challenging/experimenting with your rules, challenging/experimenting with your negative core beliefs). Have you stopped practicing these skills consistently? You may wish to revise the Sections and techniques you have learned and perhaps increase practicing those skills.

3. Social Support

    It is wise to find someone with whom you can sit down and have a good talk. This doesn't mean a therapy session where you pour out your heart but rather just a chance to talk through what's going on in your life, what your goals are, and generally just to ventilate with someone you trust. Often, problems seem bigger than they really are when a person tries to deal with them on their own. Hearing yourself talk through something can help to put it into perspective.

On the next page is a self-management plan for you to complete. Make a note of the early warning signs that might signal a setback then write down the strategies and tools you have learnt about that can help you to deal with a setback.

Self-Management Plan

What are the early warning signs that tell me that I might be heading for a setback and need to do something about it myself? Ex. I am more depressed or anxious OR I am more critical of myself OR I am expecting the worst more often OR I am *avoiding or withdrawing from things*.
What are some of my biased expectations, negative self-evaluations, unhelpful behaviors, unhelpful rules or assumptions, and negative core beliefs I need to watch out for?
If I do experience a setback, what will I do about it?
What are my future support options? *Ex, friends, family, GP, other, etc.*
What strategies/techniques have I found most helpful and need to continue to practice?
How can I build on what I have learned in this information package?

CELEBRATE!!!!!!!!!!!!!!!!!!!!!

The Sixth Stone

This is my favorite stone because of all the hard work put into the first five stones. You have gone back and forth and should be really be proud of what you have become. Finally, you are ready to let go of the past, move on, and forgive yourself. This is the point where you realize what you have gained humility. The pompous self-absorbed person is gone and in its place, is a nice, honest, and grateful person, ready to move on.

For the first time you have started judging yourself by our own standard instead of someone else's. You have begun to trust the process because you see how far you have come emotionally. You know that if you stay powerless your disease is manageable. You have grown and understand, for the first time, just like many of us, what it is to really be happy, sad, angry, or complaisant and not revert to escaping. This stone is where you will begin to not only walk the stepping stones of recovery but enjoy the challenge.

When you look at yourself and try to examine your personality, you try to figure out where the parts of your personality you don't like and the parts you are pleased with come together or are different. The parts that are problematic are the defects of your personality and you need to keep in focus that the goal is to raise awareness not to punish yourself or revert to resentments or reservations.

With the help of this manual, you will begin to understand the strength of this stone is about understanding what your needs are and the differences between your wants and your needs. This section will be all about inventories, so you can understand and set goals that are achievable.

Let's look at who we are and identify the personal issues at certain ages, (on an inventory sheet **PAGES 257-264**) identified by categories using these examples.

- Family
- Romantic Relationships
- Education
- Health
- Financial
- Friends
- Food
- Drugs
- Others

Let's now look at the above inventory and evaluate it for the issues you think you need to bring out to continue recovery.

What differences can you identify from each age group?

_____

_____

_____

_____

Now let's talk about how this inventory made you feel, looking at each of the categories.

_____

_____

_____

_____

Let's now look at the past five stones and break them down into another series of inventories **PAGES 257-264:**

- Denial
- Spiritual principals
- Reservations
- Fear
- Relationships
- Willingness
- Open-Mindedness

Now you need to look at the ability to trust and have the higher power or god of your understanding.

Are you ready for this after all the work you have done on the past stones?

_____

_____

_____

Walk the stones and see how you are doing!

Draw four stones and number them 1-4. Now decide if you are ready to toss the stone. Before you can do this, you need to reevaluate why you are ready. With each stone you toss away, "Congratulations" is in order.

Treat yourself to something special and take a break before you look at the stones five and six.

Draw stones 5 and 6. If for any reason you do not feel ready to toss a stone then please go back and redo the questions. This is not failing, it is that you are really growing and can finally be honest with yourself recognizing that there is still a lot of work to do.

This stone is attached to many emotional and spiritual threads. For some of us it is obvious and for some of us it is where we look back and realize just how much we have accomplished.

As we come to the end of this stone the final subject I would like to address is the effect of substance abuse on children.

Substance Abuse and its Effect on Children

When a parent abuses drugs or alcohol they often find it hard to be able to create nurturing relationships and a stable environment. These are critical in the development of children. This could also put your children at risk to abuse drugs themselves in the future. It is possible they will begin to view drugs as "normal behaviors" and believe drugs or alcohol can help them to deal with emotional or social problems.

You may attempt to make significant efforts to provide the stability that your children need. However, the cost of your drug use can cause you to not be able to afford the proper nutrition, clothing, and other basic needs for your children.

While using, you may not be able to deal with your child's physical or emotional needs. For example, if your child is injured while you are intoxicated and there is no one around to help you get your child to the doctor you could further endanger their lives by attempting to drive. Issues like this can lead to poor parent-child bonds. These poor bonds can lead to behavioral problems such as acting out in school.

Children who are raised with drug/alcohol abusing parents are often at a higher risk of being addicted to substances. The National Center on Addiction and Substance Abuse have researched this. The reason this occurs is that parental drug abuse creates environment stress. A teenager might abuse drugs/alcohol to deal with personal anxiety of their unstable living environment or lack of parenting. There is also a genetic component to addiction. This means that a child of a parent with addiction issues can be born predisposed to addiction.

Drug/alcohol abuse can make it hard for a parent to create routines and structure among the household. Children need routines and structure to thrive. Often, children of drug abusing parents must assume the role of parent and take care of their siblings, clean the house, or cook meals. The disciplining in the household can become inconsistent. When the regularly enforced rule, system become lax it can result in behavioral problem due to the lack of consequences.

If drug/alcohol use begin to affect your parenting it could result in child protection agencies removing your children from your home. This could result in your child being place with a relative or foster family. Removal from their home often causes trauma for your child. Even if your child is not removed from your home there is a chance your risky behaviors could lead to your arrest and incarceration. This could also majorly affect your relationship with your child(ren).

Side-Effects of Substance Abuse on Children (This is just a sampling of the different type of side-effects on children of addicted parents):

- Psychological/Emotional Reactions;
- Perpetrated illness;
- Lying;
- Bed-wetting;
- Eating Disorders;
- Inability to experience normal family relationships;
- Lack of role models (especially from men);
- Judging themselves without mercy (hard on themselves);
- Take themselves to serious, unable to be children;
- Depression and Anxiety Disorders;
- Difficulty having fun;
- Difficultly intimate relationships;
- Trust Issues;
- Terrified of abandonment;
- Easily frightened of anger;
- Consistently seeking approval; and/or
- Take responsibility above age; especially of siblings

Have your children shown any of the above side-effects of your substance related issues? If so, write about how your children have been affected.

_____

_____

_____

_____

_____

What do you do to exhibit good role-modeling for your children?

_____

_____

_____

_____

At times, children can judge themselves so harshly. What can you do to help them through the lack of self-esteem associated with this?

_____

_____

_____

_____

Children of addicted parents can have difficulty having fun. What kind of family time can/have you set aside to show your children how to have fun?

_____

_____

_____

_____

Children of addicts who grow up in this type of atmosphere deal with denial, lying and/or keeping secrets. How can you help your children develop a healthier trust system?

_____

_____

_____

_____

What is your understanding of abandonment?

How do you explain your being there or lack of being there for your children due to incarceration or separation from the home? How has or has this effected your relationship with your children? How can you improve or work on your relationship to move past this?

Perhaps you noticed your children take the role of the parent. What are you doing to help your children overcome this and become children again?

How many times have you noticed your children are frightened?

How has your substance use affected your children in school?

_____

_____

_____

_____

What holds families together is the fiber of the unit, which can sometimes be healthy or dysfunctional. Over time substance abuse can lead to a lack of boundaries in nuclear and extended family. Even with this being forgiven, families are always changing. New members of the family come in while others leave the system such as fathers, children, aunt, uncles, grandparents, and friends. These people leave their mark and role on the family unit. A family is a living system the rules and myths play a major role in the wellness of the unit.

Understanding that the family is living and ever changing is very important. The family responds to negative behaviors of chemical dependency and substance abuse often slowly overtime. This tends to become part of the everyday system. It gradually and progressively increases in both patterns of dependency and reshaping what the system looks like.

Characteristic of Children of Addicts as Adults – (Some of this section is borrowed from the Children of Alcoholics (ACOA): 13 Characteristics by Dr. Janet Woititz. Some has been rewritten to include drugs).

1. Adult children of addicts guess what normal behavior is.
   The home of addicts is not "normal." Life revolves around the addict and most family members must learn to keep their family going, as they know it. Children of alcoholics or drug addicted parents do not live the same life as their "normal" peers. Therefore, the child and later the adult must simply do their best at maintaining normalcy, as observed from friends, television or simply guessing.
2. Adult children of substance users have difficulty following a project through from beginning to end. In the home of an addict, daily living is frequently interrupted due to misbehavior or unpredictable actions of the addict. For example, the family may start playing game, but then dad comes home, and everyone must stop playing. Or maybe mom promised to help work on a school project, but then passes out and never follows through. When project completion and follow-through are not consistently modeled, it is a hard skill for the adult child of an addict to learn.
3. Adult children of an addict lie when it would be just as easy to tell the truth. As a child of an addict, one must consistently lie and make up excuses for the addicted parent. The child also hears the parent and everyone else in the family lie and make up stories constantly. This behavior is a necessity to keep the addict family intact, and therefore becomes a natural trait. Once the child acquires this behavior, it tends to stay with the adult child. These lies are not always malicious or harmful. Something as simple as the route the ACOA took home, or what type of fruit they like is fair game for lies. Unless

the child or adult receives enough consequences (either internal, like guilt or anxiety; or external, like getting in trouble with someone) the ACOA may begin to practice the art of telling the truth more.

4. Adult children of addicts judge themselves without mercy. No matter what the child of an alcoholic or addict does, they cannot "fix" their parent or their family. They may be able to take care of the addict or other members of the family, but they are unable to fix the root of the problem: the addiction and relating family dysfunction. No matter how well the child does in soccer, how high their school grades, no matter how clean they keep the house, how "good" they are, they still cannot fix the addict. Everything they do falls short. Additionally, the child of an alcoholic or addict may blame him/herself for bad things that happen in the family, and are frequently guilt-ridden for reason beyond their control. Perfectionism is very common in ACOAs.
5. Adult children of alcoholics have difficulty having fun. Growing up with an addicted parent is not fun. Kids are not allowed to be kids. When the kids are not given this joy, the adult usually does not know simply how to enjoy their life. The ACOA is constantly worrying about their addicted parent, or is in trouble for things they should not be responsible for, or compensating in some other way for the addict. The usually carefree, fun time of being a child often does not exist in the parent is an addict.
6. Adult children of addicts take themselves very seriously. Due to the gravity of their roles in their families growing up, adult children of addicts take themselves very seriously. The weight of the family, and thus the world, is on their shoulders.
7. Adult children of addicts have difficulty with intimate relationships. Having never known a "normal" relationship or family roles, the ACOA does not know how to have one. The adult child of an addict does not trust others. The ACOA has learned that people are not trustworthy or reliable, and has had their heart broken from such an early age.
8. Adult children of addicts overreact to changes over which they have no control. The child of an addict lacks control over their lives much of the time. They cannot control when their parents use, or that the parent is an addict to begin with. They cannot always predict what will happen from one day to the next, and this is very anxiety producing. A child needs to feel safe. Because of this lack of control as a child, the adult child of an addict craves control. They need to know what is going to happen, how it is going to happen, and when. Of course, this control and predictability is not always possible. If plans are changes, or somebody does something the ACOA doesn't like or feel comfortable with, all the insecurity of their childhood may come back to them, and the adult child may overreact, leaving the other party stunned or confused.
9. Adult children of addicts constantly seek approval and affirmation. Similar to ACOA characteristic number four, children of addicts are used to continuously seeking approval or praise from their parents or other valued person. They probably did not grow up with regular consistent rules and expectations, and could never make their addicted parent happy. Not knowing what is "normal" or expected, adult children of addicts need someone to tell them what they are doing is right. They are often indecisive and unsure of themselves.
10. Adult children of addicts usually feel that they are different from other people. Another overlap with other characteristics, children of addicts sometimes know from an early age that their home is not "normal." Children from addicted families may or may not

know what is different, and sometimes don't completely "get it" until they visit a friend's house and observe their parents. Consistency may be shocking, and either attacks or appalls the children who is not use to such structure.

11. Adult children of alcoholics are super responsible or super irresponsible. Once the child from an addicted family gets older and forms their own identity, the ACOA may either strictly follow a schedule and wants everything in order, controlled-perfect. These adult children often struggle with anxiety, OCD, perfectionism and eating disorders. The opposite result is the ACOA who is a "party animal." This adult child may develop an alcohol, drug or other behavioral addiction. The ACOA may live a life very much like their addicted parent, or they may "shape up" and get their life together, with the appropriate support.

12. Adult children of addicts are extremely loyal, even in the face of evidence that loyalty is undeserved. "Why do you put up with him?" Adult children of addicts are used to dealing with just that, an addict. They are used to either taking care of an addict or seeing another take care of an addict. Drunken fights and broken promises is normal or the ACOA. Growing up, the child of an addict was probably told "it isn't his fault" or "he didn't mean it, he was drunk." Because of these lowered expectations, an adult of a child of an addict frequently ends up in a relationship with another addict, abusive partner, or otherwise unhealthy relationship.

13. Adult children of alcoholics are impulsive. They tend to lock themselves into a course of actions without giving serious consideration to alternative behaviors or possible consequences. This impulsively leads to confusion, self-loathing, and loss of control over their environment. In addition, they spend an excessive amount of energy cleaning up the mess. The last trait is self-descriptive. The ACOA will struggle with falling into unhealthy patterns of behavior, in whatever form it might take. An adult child of an addict began life in an unstable, insecure environment. The ACOA did not get everything they needed from their addicted parent. These 13 ACOA characteristics may seem daunting, but they are simply a profile, description, and explanation of existing traits. These 13 characteristics are not death sentence or certainty for ACOA. Once an ACOA recognizes and understands why they are the way they are, and that they are not along, the adult child of an addict can begin to heal. With the support of a therapist, counselor, support group, and others, the ACOA can live a full, healthy life, and stop of chain of addiction.

To examine your family system and role, answer the following questions:

Do you take over the responsibilities of another member of the family, so it will get done?

_____

_____

_____

_____

Do you hide or deny any family problems?

Do you feel guilty or responsible for the actions and behaviors of others?

Have you lost your sense of self-worth in the process?

If you are a child of an addict, how did you handle this dynamic?

Have you ever avoided participating in a family dynamic?

_____

_____

_____

_____

Do you have anger or resentment towards your family?

_____

_____

_____

_____

Now is the time to really examine what change means and how it has come about in our life by just revisiting our path and the stones we have walked. We started this journey with a feeling of guilt, ashamed of our pasts, and many of us not even sure we wanted to change anything, but just wished the consequences would go away.

Arrogance and ego became replaced with confidence and gratefulness. We realized that we were only responsible for ourselves and that by really learning again to like ourselves; we could like, and even love again. And most of us learned that being powerless was wonderful. It was freeing, and we learned again how to breathe.

Now when I think of the word addiction, what do I feel?

_____

_____

_____

_____

_____

_____

The Seventh Stone

Congratulations!!!!! You have come to the final stone. It is what we call the climb back on solid ground, our ability to walk a new path knowing there are going to be many difficulties, twists, and turns. The path has taken a new direction - Recovery, what a great journey!

For those who have read previous versions of this manual you may have noticed the large amount of changes in other chapters. However, none of these changes are more significant then in Stone Seven. At this point, I have been in recovery for well over thirty (30) years and I have been in this field for about the same time. In all that time, I have discovered just like many other programs the importance of relapse prevention.

Stress is a normal reaction to the demands of life and for those newly sober it is vitally important to learn to identify and manage stress to minimize the potential for relapse. The goal of relapse prevention is to identify and reduce high risk triggers which could lead to substance use and abuse. In this section you will identify potential high-risk situations and focus on developing specific coping skills designed to help the you live a balanced and positive life free of addiction. In the remainder of this manual you will learn a variety of stimulus control and "urge management" techniques as you develop your own unique relapse prevention plan. An individual who can implement an effective coping strategy when craving or impulses occur is less likely to relapse compared with a person lacking those skills. It is for this reason that we believe in targeting the underlying behavioral health issues and place great importance on you developing the necessary skills which will lead to long-term abstinence.

Boundaries

For people in recovery, being able to set boundaries is an important skill to have. It is common for addicts to grow up in homes where boundaries are either too rigid, which leads to suppressed emotion and distant relationships or too enmeshed, which takes away their sense of personal identity. Later in life it is more likely for them to maintain these types of relationships; making depression, anxiety, and addictive behavior more likely.

Part of recovery is learning how to set boundaries and how to respects other's boundaries; this is often referred to as embracing the authentic self. This is a process of finding out who you want to be, how you want to interact with others, and how to take responsibility for your actions.

Boundaries are important because they protect you from being manipulated, abused, or taken advantage of; they also protect others from harm you may cause. When you have healthy boundaries in place, it allows you to listen and trust your own thoughts and feelings and communicate those to others.

Distinguishing Healthy and Unhealthy Boundaries

Healthy boundaries are not trying to control and manipulate others into doing what you want, or rules designed to shut people out or hide your feelings. Healthy boundaries are simply an outline of how you want to be treated and the results that come from not following the boundaries. People with healthy boundaries normally feel a sense control for their own behavior, are able to manage the effects of their behavior and decisions, can express their thoughts and feelings, and say no when needed. People with unhealthy boundaries put aside their goals, values and plans to satisfy others, allow others to tell them who they are and what to do, expect other people to take care of their needs, can't say no, aren't confident with their own opinions, feel mistreated by others, and feel that other's problems are their fault.

Unhealthy boundaries can lead to lower self-esteem, and a higher chance of codependency, victimization, and behavioral obsession. In summary those that set strong boundaries don't have to worry about the unpredictability of their environment because they are ready for it.

Steps to create healthy boundaries: identify your own feelings, values and beliefs, set limits based on your feelings, beliefs and values, speak up when your limits are being pushed, listen to yourself and respect other's boundaries.

Examples of Healthy and Unhealthy Boundaries

Healthy- the ability to express your thoughts and feelings, the ability to respects other's values and opinions, the ability to respect your own values and opinions despite what other think, the ability to take responsibility for your own actions

Unhealthy- discouraging other's values and opinions, forcing your values and opinions onto others, disregarding your values and opinion because of others, allowing other people to tell you what to do and who you should be, and taking responsibility for other's emotions.

Why do Addicts Have Unhealthy Boundaries?

Addicts generally create unhealthy boundaries because of neglect from guardians or strict, over-bearing guardians. Guardians that neglect their children care about what others think of their children and don't care to see any problems the child might be facing. They don't put any boundaries in place, so the child doesn't learn anything about social interaction. Neglected children learn to be independent at an early age, avoid close relationships and keep emotions hidden, which can lead them to look to drugs and alcohol to release these emotions. Strict, over-bearing guardians give their children too many boundaries, which don't allow them any room for personal growth and creates dependency problems. Most addicts show characteristics of dependency and little understanding of boundaries.

Defining Your Boundaries

Boundaries allow you to manage your environment. The places you go, people you associate with and events you attend all effect your life in some way; boundaries help you decide the degree to which they affect your life. Boundaries cannot be seen so it is your job to define your boundaries.

Consistency is one of the most important components in setting boundaries; you have to set consistent and clear-cut boundaries that are not affected by other people. Your boundaries can be flexible, but they should only change because you want them to. By setting these consistent, clear-cut boundaries, you will create an environment where you are able to trust in yourself.

Having heathy boundaries is important because without them you can question your own value system, which leads to emotional instability and at the root of all problems, is emotional instability. Because life changes so much, your boundaries will to, but it's your responsibility to keep your needs ahead of everything else.

Active Listening

Active listening entails the listener to have full concentration, an understanding of what is being said and a response to what is being said. Active listening should be used in counseling. Active listening can help people feel more comfortable with opening their emotions, avoid any misunderstandings, resolve issues, and build trust.

There are some barriers to active listening; including: the language the speaker uses, trigger words, vocabulary, limited attention span and distractions. To overcome these barriers, you need to put personal opinions aside, ask questions about things you don't understand and paraphrase what the speaker said to make sure you both have the same idea, stay focused, maintain eye contact and use appropriate body language.

Comprehension

The first step to active listening is comprehension. Comprehension is a mutual understanding of what is being said by the speaker.

Retaining

The second step in active listening is retention. The meaning of the conversation is created through the information you retain.

Responding

The third step in active listening is responding. Listening is the interaction between the person speaking and the listener, therefore you need to respond.

Tactic

The forth step in active listening is to pay attention to the speaker's behavior and body language. Observing the body language of the speaker allows the listener to get a better understanding of the speakers point.

What Are Personal Boundaries?

Personal boundaries are the limits and rules we set for ourselves within relationships. A person with healthy boundaries can say "no" to others when they want to, but they are also comfortable opening themselves up to intimacy and close relationships. A person who always keeps others at a distance (whether emotionally, physically, or otherwise) is said to have rigid boundaries. Alternatively, someone who tends to get too involved with others has porous boundaries.

Common traits of rigid, porous, and healthy boundaries.

Rigid Boundaries	Porous Boundaries	Healthy Boundaries
• Avoids intimacy and close relationships. • Unlikely to ask for help. Has few close relationships. • Very protective of personal information. • May seem detached, even with romantic partners. • Keeps others at a distance to avoid the possibility of rejection.	• Overshares personal information. • Difficulty saying "no" to the requests of others. Overinvolved with other's problems. • Dependent on the opinions of others. • Accepting of abuse or disrespect. • Fears rejection if they do not comply with others.	• Values own opinions. • Doesn't compromise values for others. • Shares personal information in an appropriate way (does not over or under share). Knows personal wants and needs, and can communicate them. • Accepting when others say "no" to them.

Most people have a mix of different boundary types. For example, someone could have healthy boundaries at work, porous boundaries in romantic relationships, and a mix of all three types with their family. One size does not fit all!

The appropriateness of boundaries depends heavily on setting. What's appropriate to say when you're out with friends might not be appropriate when you're at work.

Some cultures have very different expectations when it comes to boundaries. For example, in some cultures it's considered wildly inappropriate to express emotions publicly. In other cultures, emotional expression is encouraged.

Types of Boundaries

Physical boundaries refer to personal space and physical touch. Healthy physical boundaries include an awareness of what's appropriate, and what's not, in various settings and types of relationships (hug, shake hands, or kiss?). Physical boundaries may be violated if someone touches you when you don't want them to, or when they invade your personal space (for example, rummaging through your bedroom).

Intellectual boundaries refer to thoughts and ideas. Healthy intellectual boundaries include respect for others' ideas, and an awareness of appropriate discussion (should we talk about the weather, or politics?). Intellectual boundaries are violated when someone dismisses or belittles another person's thoughts or ideas.

Emotional boundaries refer to a person's feelings. Healthy emotional boundaries include limitations on when to share, and when not to share, personal information. For example, gradually sharing personal information during the development of a relationship, as opposed to revealing everything to everyone. Emotional boundaries are violated when someone criticizes, belittles, or invalidates another person's feelings.

Sexual boundaries refer to the emotional, intellectual, and physical aspects of sexuality. Healthy sexual boundaries involve mutual understanding and respect of limitations and desires between sexual partners. Sexual boundaries can be violated with unwanted sexual touch, pressure to engage in sexual acts, leering, or sexual comments.

Material boundaries refer to money and possessions. Healthy material boundaries involve setting limits on what you will share, and with whom. For example, it may be appropriate to lend a car to a family member, but probably not to someone you met this morning. Material boundaries are violated when someone steals or damages another person's possessions, or when they pressure them to give or lend them their possessions.

Time boundaries refer to how a person uses their time. To have healthy time boundaries, a person must set aside enough time for various facets of their lives such as work, relationships, and hobbies. Time boundaries are violated when another person demands too much of another's time

How do I Communicate my Boundaries to Other People?

Here are some words to use:
- I have a problem with that
- I don't want to
- I've decided not to
- This is what I need
- This hard for me to say
- Understand your point of view but
- I feel uncomfortable about
- I'd rather not
- Yes, I do mind
- I'd prefer not to
- It's important to me
- I'll think about it
- That's unacceptable
- I guess we see it differently

Who do I need to establish clear boundaries with?

_____

_____

_____

_____

Personal boundaries are rules or limits that a person creates for themselves. Boundaries are reasonable and safe ways for other people to behave around you and a guide to how you should behave around others. In the box below are a list of personal boundaries.

Kiss, Shake hands, Hold hands, Hug, Wave, Say "Hi", Fist bump, Say "I love you", Text, Tell secrets, Talk about personal issues, Enter their home, Give your phone number, Give your address, Chat on a computer, Say "Thank you"

List some boundaries that are acceptable in each group below:

Family: _____

_____

_____

Acquaintances: _____

_____

_____

Strangers: _____

_____

_____

Peer Pressure

Peer pressure can affect anyone, no matter what their age, and makes it very difficult to resist the urges to use drugs. To battle against peer pressure, you need to know how to identify it. People give into peer pressure for two main reasons: they are uncertain about how to get out of an uncomfortable situation or they want to be a part of the crowd. There are many types of peer pressure and some of them may not feel dangerous at the beginning. Having the ability to identify when someone is peer pressuring helps to fight against it and stay sober long term.

How to Prepare for Peer Pressure Situations

One way to fight against peer pressure is to practice responses to decline offers to use drugs or practice excuses to leave an uncomfortable situation. Another way to fight against peer pressure is to invite someone you know will stay sober to serve as indirect support. While in many situations family members and friends understand your situation after you explain it, there are situations where family and friends continue to be a source of peer pressure. In this circumstance you need to either limit the time you spend with them or cut them out of your life entirely. While this may seem harsh it is necessary for your sobriety. One of the best ways to resist peer pressure is to get involved in a new social group with other that are sober. Athletic pursuits often influence addicts to stay sober because to be your best, you need to remain sober. No matter what you do the point is to get involved with something to keep you busy and away from drugs. The number one best way to stay away from peer pressure is to seek professional help. Professional help can give people techniques to resist the pressure on an ongoing basis.

Different Types of Peer Pressure

Peer Pressure Masked by Hospitality

While addicts really shouldn't take part in social events where there is drinking, there are situations where there are not avoidable. Often host feel that they are being bad host if their guest can't relax with a drink, so they tend to be a little pushy without meaning to. One way to remove yourself from this situation is to change the subject to something you're enjoying at the party to show the host that you are having good time without drinking. A way to prevent this from even happening is to bring your own beverage.

Peer Pressure Masked by Nosiness

Because people don't fully understand what you are going though they might have many questions; questions that you are not required to answer. If someone seems trustworthy to you, feel free to be open and explain your disease, but if they start asking questions you aren't comfortable with or questions that clearly resemble peer pressure, you can remove yourself from the situation.

Peer Pressure in The Purest Form

There are people that will try to peer pressure you, and what makes it worse is that it is not always easy to tell who those people are. Through therapy you can learn how to not let peer pressure take away your control and sobriety.

> **Quick tips on resisting pressure**
>
> Say no and let them know you mean it.
>
> - Stand up straight
> - Make eye contact
> - Say how you feel
> - Don't make excuses
> - Stick up for yourself

Friends (or peers) can have a good or bad influence on you. A bad influence, for example, is that friends at school may ask you to join in a game to be nasty to other friends just for fun. Another friend might try to make you post a nasty picture on Instagram or write nasty comments on Facebook. You may end up doing things you regret to impress your friends, although you know that it is wrong. These situations are all examples of negative pee pressure.

Peer pressure happens when people want to be loved and accepted by others. It is easier to be swayed to do things that wouldn't normally do if you're in a crowd. Some people think that "if everyone else is doing it so why shouldn't I" but this can make sensible people behave in strange ways. Answer the following:

How would you define a good friend?

_____

_____

_____

_____

What is your own understating of peer pressure?

_____

_____

_____

Has anyone ever tried to put you under pressure to do things that you would not normally do? Elaborate.

___

___

___

___

How did the above make you feel?

___

___

___

___

Do your friends accept you if you have the opinion of your own? If no, elaborate.

___

___

___

___

Anger

Anger is a strong feeling of annoyance, displeasure, or hostility. Anger that is persistent and has gotten stronger over a period is resentment. By allowing anger to fester into resentment and not recognizing the fault you had in a situation, it puts you at risk to blame your bad choices on others. It makes you avoid the fact that you are responsible for your own choices and can overall lead to relapse. When you begin to feel anger, you should: breath, identify your feelings and why you're having those feelings and talk to someone you feel comfortable with. When you have feelings of resentment it is important for you to recognize your part in the situation, by doing this you learn what you can control and what you need to change.

When you hold anger in, it can lead to outburst, which can cause friendships and families to fall apart. When you are angry it causes you to act impulsively and not think clearly, which can lead to criminal activities such as breaking and entering, stealing, and vandalizing property. If you learn how to control your anger it gives you more control over your emotions and actions. If you don't learn how to manage your anger it increases your chance of relapse.

Anger Management Skills

Recognize your Anger Early	If you're yelling, it's probably too late. Learn the warning signs that you're getting angry so you can change the situation quickly. Some common signs are feeling hot, raising voices, balling of fists, shaking, and arguing.
Take a Timeout	Temporarily leave the situation that is making you angry. If other people are involved, explain to them that you need a few minutes alone to calm down. Problems usually aren't solved when one or more people are angry.
Deep Breathing	Take a minute to just breathe. Count your breaths: four seconds inhaling, four seconds holding your breath, and four seconds exhaling. Really keep track of time, or you might cheat yourself! The counting helps take your mind off the situation as well.
Exercise	Exercise serves as an emotional release. Chemicals released in your brain during the course of exercise create a sense of relaxation and happiness.
Express your Anger	Once you've calmed down, express your frustration. Try to be assertive, but not confrontational. Expressing your anger will help avoid the same problems in the future.
Think of the Consequences	What will be the outcome of your next anger-fueled action? Will arguing convince the other person that you're right? Will you be happier after the fight?
Visualization	Imagine a relaxing experience. What do you see, smell, hear, feel, and taste? Maybe you're on a beach with sand between your toes and waves crashing in the distance. Spend a few minutes imagining every detail of your relaxing scene.

Introduction to Anger Management

 Anger: a strong feeling of annoyance, displeasure, or hostility
Aggression: hostile or violent behavior or attitudes toward another

Feelings of anger are a normal and healthy part of being human. Learning to avoid all anger would be an impossible goal. Instead, in anger management, you will learn to avoid negative reactions to anger (such as aggression), while learning new healthy habits.

The first step in anger management is to begin learning about your own anger. To start, you will learn about triggers (the things that set you off), how you respond to anger, and how anger has affected your life.

List three situations, topics, or people that often leads to you feeling angry:
(ex. arguing with your partner about money, dealing with authority, poor drivers)

What do you *do* when you're angry? List ways in which you act differently when angry:
(ex. shouting, arguing, throwing or breaking objects, become physically aggressive)

Have you ever run into problems because of your anger? If so, list them:
(ex. damaged relationships, reprimanded at work, public altercations)

Anger Warning Signs

Sometimes anger can affect what you say or do before you even recognize the feeling. This is especially true if you feel angry all the time. You may become so used to the feeling of anger that you don't notice it, sort of like how you can hear the sound of an air condition or the humming of a refrigerator but block it from your mind. Even if you aren't thinking about your feelings, they influence how you behave. The first step to managing anger is learning to recognize your personal warning signs that tell you how you feel.

How do you react when you feel angry? Some of these warning signs might start when you are only a little irritated, and others might start when you are very angry. Circle the warning signs that apply to you.

Mind goes blank	Insult the other person	Face turns red
Body or hands shake	Start sweating	Throw things
Heavy or fast breathing	Stare at the other person	Scowl or make an angry face
Scream, raise voice, or yell	Clench fists	Feel sick to the stomach
Punch walls	Feel hot	Become aggressive
Become argumentative	Go quiet and "shut down"	Crying
Pace around the room	Headaches	Can't stop thinking about the problem

How I Feel

I feel: _____

Happy	Mad	Sad	Glad
Worried	Excited	Bored	Scared
Annoyed	Upset	Sick	Nervous

I feel this way because:

_____
_____
_____

This is what I did about it:

_____
_____
_____

Something else I could have done is:

_____
_____
_____

Ask for help	Take deep breaths	Walk away
Do something else	Tell an adult	Talk to a friend

Anger Diary

Anger has a way of sneaking up and taking control of our thoughts and actions before we realize what is happening. Fortunately, with practice, you can get better at catching your anger long before it takes over. Keeping an anger diary will help you achieve that goal.

Instructions: Either at the end of the day, or a few hours after your anger has passed, take a moment to reflect on a situation where you felt angry, or even just a bit frustrated. By following the example, take a few notes about the event. After recording five events, complete the review.

Example

Triggers	"My husband tracked mud all over the carpet and didn't even notice. I had just mopped a few days ago, so I lost it."
Warning signs	"Before I got angry, I noticed that my hands were shaking, and I was argumentative. Then, as I got angrier, my face felt really hot."
Anger Response	"I screamed at my husband. I wanted to throw something, but I didn't. I couldn't stop thinking about how selfish he is."
Outcome	"My husband ended up getting really angry too, and we argued for hours. It was miserable. I went to bed feeling guilty and sad."

Event One

Triggers	
Warning signs	
Anger Response	
Outcome	

Event Two

Triggers	
Warning signs	
Anger Response	
Outcome	

Event Three

Triggers	
Warning signs	
Anger Response	
Outcome	

Event Four

Triggers	
Warning signs	
Anger Response	
Outcome	

Event Five

Triggers	
Warning signs	
Anger Response	
Outcome	

Review

Do you notice any patterns related to your anger?	
Generally, how would you like to react differently?	

Trauma

Trauma is an emotional response to a tragic event. Most people who struggle with drug/alcohol addiction have experienced trauma in their life time. Trauma can lead to deep trust issues, guilt, shame, etc., which some try to mask with drugs and alcohol. While self-medicating can be effective, it often leads to the cycle of addiction. Common causes of trauma are: sexual assault, natural disasters, a victim of crime, witness of crime/death, loss of a loved one, childhood abuse, physical abuse, emotional abuse, or chronic illness. The symptoms of trauma can be crippling and can prevent people from moving on with daily life and responsibilities. Symptoms of trauma are: anger, depression, anxiety, paranoia, high stress levels, sadness, mood swings and exhaustion. If you are struggling with trauma it is important you seek counseling to comfort, learn about and heal from the trauma.

Life Story the Past, Present, and Future

Writing a story about your life can help you find meaning and value in your experiences. It will allow you to organize your thoughts and use them to grow. People who develop stories about their life tend to experience a greater sense of meaning, which can contribute to happiness.

The Past

Write the story of your past. Be sure to describe challenges you've overcome, and the personal strengths that allowed you to do so.

_____

_____

_____

_____

_____

_____

_____

_____

_____

_____

The Present

Describe your life and who you are now. How do you differ from your past self? What are your strengths now? What challenges are you facing?

_____

_____

_____

_____

_____

_____

_____

_____

The Future

Write about your ideal future. How will your life be different than it is now? How will you be different than you are now?

_____

_____

_____

_____

_____

_____

_____

Anxiety and other Dual Diagnosed Conditions Test

Yes ○ No ○	Over the last several months, heave you be continually worried or anxious about many events or activities in your daily life?

Are you troubled by the following?

Yes ○ No ○	Excessive worry, occurring more days than not, for a least six months
Yes ○ No ○	Unreasonable worry about events or activities, such as work, school, or your health
Yes ○ No ○	The inability to control the worry

Are you bothered by at least three of the following?

Yes ○ No ○	Restlessness, feeling keyed-up, or on edge
Yes ○ No ○	Being easily tired
Yes ○ No ○	Problems concentrating
Yes ○ No ○	Irritability
Yes ○ No ○	Muscle tension
Yes ○ No ○	Trouble falling or staying asleep, or restless and unsatisfying sleep
Yes ○ No ○	Your anxiety interfering with your daily life

Having more than one illness at the same time can make it difficult to diagnose and treat the different conditions. Depression and substance abuse are among the conditions that occasionally complicate anxiety disorders.

Yes ○ No ○	Have you experienced changes in sleeping or eating habits?

More days than not, do you feel

Yes ○ No ○	Sad or depressed?
Yes ○ No ○	Disinterested in life?
Yes ○ No ○	Worthless or guilty?

During the last year, has the use of alcohol or drugs...

Yes ○ No ○	Resulted in your failure to fulfill responsibilities with work, school, or family?
Yes ○ No ○	Placed you in a dangerous situation, such as driving a car under the influence?
Yes ○ No ○	Gotten you arrested?
Yes ○ No ○	Continued despite causing problems for you or your loved ones?

Challenging Anxious Thoughts

Anxiety can be a healthy emotion—it forces us to focus on our problems, and work hard to solve them. But sometimes, anxiety grows out of control, and does just the opposite. It cripples our ability to solve problems. When this happens, irrational thoughts often play a role. In this exercise, we will practice catching our irrational thoughts, and replacing them with rational alternatives. With enough practice, this will become a natural process that can help you manage anxiety.

Describe a common situation that triggers your anxiety: example: "giving a speech in front of a crowd" or "driving in rush hour traffic"

Anxiety distorts our thinking by causing us to overestimate the likelihood of something going wrong, and imagine the potential consequences as worse than they really are. Sometimes, just taking a moment to think about these facts can help us recognize our irrational thoughts.

Imagine you are faced with the anxiety-producing situation from above. Describe the…

Worst Outcome:
Best Outcome:
Likely Outcome:

Imagine the worst outcome comes true. Would it still matter…

1 week from now:
1 month from now:
1 year from now:

Usually, anxious thoughts focus on the worst possible outcomes, even when they aren't likely. For example, a person who is nervous about giving a speech might think: "I am going to forget everything and embarrass myself, and I'll never live it down". As an outside observer, we know that an alternate, more rational thought might be: "My speech might only be OK, but if I do mess up, everyone will forget about it soon enough".

Using your own "worst outcome" and "likely outcome" from above, describe your…

Irrational Thought:
Rational Thought:

Panic Assessment

What were you thinking about before your most recent panic attack?

_____

_____

_____

_____

_____

How were you feeling before your most recent panic attack?

_____

_____

_____

_____

_____

_____

What were you doing before your most recent panic attack?

_____

_____

_____

_____

Circle the symptoms you experience during panic attacks

Pounding or racing heart	Difficulty breathing	Sweating
Sense of terror, impending doom, or death	Feeling dizzy, light-headed, or faint	Feeling of being detached from reality or oneself
Fear of "going crazy"	Nausea	Chest pain or discomfort
Choking sensation	Chills or feeling of heat	Numbness or tingling
Trembling or shaking	Other	

Are you worried about having another panic attack?

Not Worried				Very Worried
1	2	3	4	5

How would you rate the discomfort caused by your panic attacks?

No Discomfort 1	2	3	4	Very Uncomfortable 5

Have you changed your behavior because of your past panic attacks? Example: Avoiding situations that you think might cause a panic attack, or places where a panic attack would be embarrassing or dangerous.

_____

_____

_____

_____

_____

_____

_____

_____

_____

Relaxation Techniques

When a person is confronted with anxiety, their body undergoes several changes and enters a special state called the fight-or-flight response. The body prepares to either fight or flee the perceived danger. During the fight-or-flight response it's common to experience a "blank" mind, increased heart rate, sweating, tense muscles, and more. Unfortunately, these bodily responses do little good when it comes to protecting us from modern sources of anxiety. Using a variety of skills, you can end the fight-or-flight response before the symptoms become too extreme. These skills will require practice to work effectively, so don't wait until the last minute to try them out!

Deep Breathing It's natural to take long, deep breaths, when relaxed. However, during the fight-or-flight response, breathing becomes rapid and shallow. Deep breathing reverses that, and sends messages to the brain to begin calming the body. Practice will make your body respond more efficiently to deep breathing in the future.

Breathe in slowly. Count in your head and make sure the inward breath lasts at least 5 seconds. Pay attention to the feeling of the air filling your lungs.
Hold your breath for 5 to 10 seconds (again, keep count). You don't want to feel uncomfortable, but it should last quite a bit longer than an ordinary breath.
Breathe out very slowly for 5 to 10 seconds (count!). Pretend like you're breathing through a straw to slow yourself down. Try using a real straw to practice.
Repeat the breathing process until you feel calm.

Imagery

Think about some of your favorite and least favorite places. If you think about the place hard enough—if you really try to think about what it's like—you may begin to have feelings you associate with that location. Our brain can create emotional reactions based entirely off of our thoughts. The imagery technique uses this to its advantage.

Make sure you're somewhere quiet without too much noise or distraction. You'll need a few minutes to just spend quietly, in your mind.
Think of a place that's calming for you. Some examples are the beach, hiking on a mountain, relaxing at home with a friend, or playing with a pet.

Paint a picture of the calming place in your mind. Don't just think of the place briefly—imagine every little detail. Go through each of your senses and imagine what you would experience in your relaxing place. Here's an example using a beach:

   a. Sight: The sun is high in the sky and you're surrounded by white sand. There's no one else around. The water is a greenish-blue and waves are calmly rolling in from the ocean.
   b. Sound: You can hear the deep pounding and splashing of the waves. There are seagulls somewhere in the background.
   c. Touch: The sun is warm on your back, but a breeze cools you down just enough. You can feel sand moving between my toes.
   d. Taste: You have a glass of lemonade that's sweet, tart, and refreshing.
   e. Smell: You can smell the fresh ocean air, full of salt and calming aromas.

Progressive Muscle Relaxation

During the fight-or-flight response, the tension in our muscles increases. This can lead to a feeling of stiffness, or even back and neck pain. Progressive muscle relaxation teaches us to become more aware of this tension, so we can better identify and address stress.

Find a private and quiet location. You should sit or lie down somewhere comfortable.

The idea of this technique is to intentionally tense each muscle, and then to release the tension. Let's practice with your feet.

a. Tense the muscles in your toes by curling them into your foot. Notice how it feels when your foot is tense. Hold the tension for 5 seconds.
b. Release the tension from your toes. Let them relax. Notice how your fingers feel differently after you release the tension.
c. Tense the muscles all throughout your calf. Hold it for 5 seconds. Notice how the feeling of tension in your leg feels.
d. Release the tension from your calf, and notice how the feeling of relaxation differs.

Follow this pattern of tensing and releasing tension all throughout your body. After you finish with your feet and legs, move up through your torso, arms, hands, neck, and head.

Triggers

Triggers are events that lead to panic, anger, despair, or anxiety. To stay sober you need to learn how to identify your triggers and learn how to cope with them because if you don't learn to control them they can lead to relapse. The people, places and things from addict's past can all be triggers that lead to relapse.

There are three categories of triggers: environmental, re-exposure and stress. Environmental triggers normally include events that they associate with their drug use. Re-exposure triggers are when a recovering addict is put in a situation where they are around drugs. Stress triggers occur in circumstances that include anger, fear, anxiety, and sadness. Everyday stress that "normal" people can handle may be too hard for addicts to handle which therefore leads them to relapse. These stimuli can cause intense cravings for drugs that you won't be able to control without the correct tools.

Examples of Triggers

- Financial issues
- Losing a relationship
- Being criticized
- Family issues
- Drug/ alcohol commercials
- Feeling of being overwhelmed
- Trauma (death)
- Sights, sounds or smells
- Certain people or places

Triggers Worksheet

Trigger: A stimulus – such as a person, place, situation, or thing – that contributes to an unwanted emotional behavioral response.

The Problem

Describe the problem your triggers are contributing to. What's the worst-case scenario, if you are exposed to your triggers?

Trigger Categories

Just about anything can be a trigger. To begin exploring your own triggers, think about each of the categories listed below. Is there a specific emotion that acts as a trigger for you? How about a person or place? List your responses in the provided places.

Emotional State	
People	
Places	
Things	
Thoughts	
Activities/Situations	

Tips for Dealing with Triggers

Oftentimes, the best way to deal with a trigger is to avoid it. This might mean making changes to your lifestyle, relationships, or daily routine.

Create a strategy to deal with your triggers head on, just in case. Your strategy might include coping skills, a list of trusted people you can talk to, or rehearsed phrases to help your get out of a troublesome situation.

Don't wait on the heat of the moment to test your coping strategy. Practice!

In this section you will develop a plan for dealing with your three biggest triggers. Review your plan regularly, and practice each strategy.

Described your three biggest triggers, in detail.

Trigger 1	
Trigger 2	
Trigger 3	

Describe your strategy for avoiding or reducing exposure to each trigger.

Trigger 1	
Trigger 2	
Trigger 3	

Describe your strategy for dealing with each trigger head on, when they cannot be avoided.

Trigger 1	
Trigger 2	
Trigger 3	

Decision Making

7 Steps to Effective Decision Making:

Using a step-by-step process to make decisions, makes your decisions purposeful and well thought out and increases the chance that you will pick the better choice.

- Step 1: Analyze the Decision
- Step 2: Collect all Relevant Information
- You will either get this information thought self-evaluation or external sources such as: books, other people, online, etc.
- Step 3: Identify all Choices
- In most circumstances as you gather information you will realize that there are many different choices; you need to identify all these choices.
- Step 4: Examine the Evidence
- Using the information, you gathered, and your emotion identify the consequences of

each choice and examine how they I would each affect you. After you have done this put the choices in order from most desirable to least.
- Step 5: Make a choice
- Choose which option fits your needs and resources best.
- Step 6: Act
- Step 7: Reevaluate your Decision and its consequences

Evaluate whether your decision fixed the problem, if it hasn't you should go back over the steps.

Decision Making Worksheet

Define the question: What are you trying to decide?

_____

_____

_____

_____

Research the facts: Research your opinion to decide on facts.

_____

_____

_____

_____

Compare pros and cons for each option.

_____

_____

_____

_____

Complete the Decision-Making Chart

Define Question: _____	
(What is the question you are trying to answer?)	
Pros	**Cons**

Prevention

Relapse prevention tools are strategies that help you stay sober after leaving a treatment center. A good relapse prevention plan starts even before temptation occurs, and includes plans for social interaction and emotional triggers and positive coping mechanisms. Addiction tends to isolate individuals, but recovery is not a solo job; it requires support from others around you. When you have a support group you gain assistance, reduce stress in social situations, develop positive relationship with others that won't enable your drug use, and empower yourself. Studies show that men relapse more than women because women tend to seek help more than men.

Steps to creating a prevention plan:
- Use an index card, so it's easy to carry around
- Create a list of the people you can call when needed on one side
- Create a list of things to do other than use drugs on the other side

Tools to prevent relapse:

- Avoidance is a good tool to keep you out of situations that could influence your relapse. If you feel that you can't avoid a situation it is a good idea to consider taking a close friend or family member that will influence you to stay away from your drug.

- Self-assessment is the ability to realize the situation you're in and whether it could lead you to relapse.
- Attending Counseling Groups is one of the best tools to prevent relapse and come back from a relapse. It allows you to share your experiences with others that can relate to them and possibly offer you advice to work through your problems. Support groups also provide structured programs to follow that can make staying sober easier.
- Replacing your addiction with something more positive alternatives can also help you stay away from relapsing. Some examples of substitutions are exercise, spending time with family, working, furthering your education, etc. Try to keep yourself busy.
- Monitoring your stress levels is an important tool to stay sober; it is important that in times of negativity you try to look on the bright side and seek help where it's needed.

Mistakes Happen

It is important to realize that mistakes do happen. Studies have shown that 40 to 60 percent of recovering addicts relapse at some time during their recovery journey. But it is imperative that you immediately seek treatment, so you can continue your road to recovery.

<u>Revisiting Reservations</u>

Revisit the following section from Stone Three and without comparing them to your prior answers, answer the following questions again. Once complete go back to compare them to your prior answers.

Reservation is an unstated doubt that prevents you from accepting something wholeheartedly. It gives you an excuse to come back or repeat a negative thought or behavior (relapse). When we go to a hotel we make a reservation and that is to hold a room for us as we plan to use it upon arrival of a given time and date. Well, we do the same thing subconsciously when we reserve the right to relapse. When we bargain with our disease such as; "maybe after a while I can drink again", "I can still hang out, just not use", "I only go to the bar to play pool", "it's my sister so if she still uses pills that's not me", "after my probation or when all my court fines are paid and probation or DUI sanctions are met I can do anything I want as an adult". We tell ourselves that again we know how to do it better this time, so we go forward.

Have you really understood the concept of this program and that this is a disease?

_____

_____

_____

What are the situations that I thought or convinced myself were acceptable to get high or drink over and when and why?

___

I know other people who now drink socially or smoke a joint occasionally. I believe I can also do this. Why?

___

Do I believe with all the work I have done on myself I can now control my using?

___

How is this different from every other time you went back to thinking you had control over this disease?

_____

_____

_____

_____

_____

_____

Surrender

Revisit the following section from Stone Three and without comparing them to your prior answers, answer the following questions again. Once complete go back to compare them to your prior answers.

<u>Surrender</u> means to relinquish the control over, not giving up in weakness but just being finished with the fight. When one army surrenders to another they refuse to fight any longer. When we surrender to the disease of addiction we are accepting that we cannot control this, and we just need to accept it.

It is a great mental relief to be done and look back at our definitions and see how powerless we are over our compulsive racing thoughts. What is the difference between resigning to a situation and surrendering? Well it's all about being done.

When I reserve a room, I don't own it. I just want to use it for a while but when I surrender I am finished. I own the responsibility for whatever reason I finally get it. I am ready to lay down my pride and my selfishness. I have no more fight in me. I put up my white flag and this is where my recovery begins.

I accept that I can never do it the same way. If I have failed before I now reserve the right to try again each time I surrender. I may not be sure of how to play this

New game of life but I know it will be by new rules. It's not about the game any longer, it's about me and what's important in my life.

To complete, determine if you understand this currently. It is important to sit down and write every possible reason or fear you can think of that keeps you from completely surrendering to the disease concept of addiction (friends, family, change, etc.).

This is a great place to do another inventory. Do this inventory using your categories and

GO TO: INVENTORY LOCATED ON PAGES 257-264

What would my life be like if I surrender to the concept that I have a disease and that it is about how I think?

_____

_____

_____

_____

What will my life and the life of the people I touch be like if I don't surrender, and continue the way I have been going with compulsive and obsessiveness of my thinking that dictates my actions?

_____

_____

_____

_____

At this point you need to see if you've only gotten sober or if you are ready to embrace recovery. Write your thoughts.

_____

_____

_____

_____

The following pages are worksheets and tips on building your own relapse prevention plan:

Relapse Prevention Plan

Coping Skills: List activities or skills you enjoy that can get your mind off of using.

1	
2	
3	

Social Support: Who are three people you can talk to if you are thinking about using?

1	
2	
3	

Consequences: How will your life change if you relapse? How about if you stay sober?

Outcomes of Relapse	Outcomes of Sobriety

Tips to avoid relapse:

- Cravings will eventually pass. Do your best to distract yourself and ride it out.
- Don't become complacent. Relapse can happen years after you've quit using. It probably won't ever be safe to "just have one".
- Avoid situations that you know will put you at risk of relapse, such as spending time with friends who use drugs or going places that remind you of your past use.
- The decision to relapse is made when you put yourself in risky situations, long before you actually use.
- Don't view relapse as a failure. Falling back into old patterns because of a slip will only make the situation worse.

Avoiding Relapse

If I were about to relapse, here is a likely situation I might be in:

Where: _____

When: _____

With whom: _____

Doing what: _____

Thinking what: _____

Feeling what: _____

What coping strategies could I use to avoid this relapse?

Action Strategies:

1) _____

2) _____

3) _____

Thinking Strategies:

1) _____

2) _____

3) _____

Feeling Strategies:

1) _____

2) _____

3) _____

My Relapse Prevention Plan

Times of high risk:

e.g. Christmas

Warning signs & combating them:

Early warning sign	Thought? Behaviour?	Challenge it!	Develop a plan
e.g. skipping meals	behaviour	I know that skipping meals makes me more likely to binge	Keep to regular eating, even though I'll be eating more at Xmas

Dealing with setbacks:

Lapse behaviour	What lead to the lapse?	What could I do differently in the future?	What do I need to do to get back on track?
e.g. Binged and purged	Not sure – restricting? Skipped a meal?	Regular eating. Remember, both 'everyday' foods & 'occasional' foods are OK	Eat regularly, eat mindfully, eat slowly. Put food on plate first

Relapse Prevention Plan

Five warning signs that I might use:

1.

2.

3.

4.

5.

Five people who I can call to help me get through a craving:

1.

2.

3.

4.

5.

Five things I can do to get my mind off of using:

1.

2.

3.

4.

5.

Positive Experiences

Write briefly about times when you have displayed each of the following qualities.

❖ **Courage**

❖ **Kindness**

❖ **Selflessness**

❖ **Love**

❖ **Sacrifice**

❖ **Wisdom**

❖ **Happiness**

❖ **Determination**

Relapse Prevention Plan

Relapse Signature

Mental illness comes in many forms, and everybody's experience of mental illness is different. The term "relapse signature" refers to the specific thoughts, feelings and behaviours that you experience when you are becoming unwell. Recognising the signature will give to time to get the help you need when you need it.

Thoughts ➡

Feelings ➡

Behaviours ➡

Staying Well

It is now widely accepted that unwanted stress can contribute to mental illness, and therefore stress needs to be managed and limited. Identifying stressors is the first step to managing them.

My Stressors ➡

What can I do about them? ➡

How will I change my life? ➡

If I begin to feel unwell, I will ➡

Tips for Avoiding Relapse

The most important moment before relapse isn't the final decision to use a drug. It's when you decide to expose yourself to triggers. For example, a trigger could be going to a party or walking through the liquor section at the store. Before encountering your triggers, *you* still have most of the control. Not your craving.

If you're feeling the urge to use, try to wait it out. If you distract yourself for even 30 minutes, it's likely your craving will lessen in intensity. It might not totally disappear, but it will become easier to resist.

Focus on replacing your past drug use with new positive activities. If you used to go home after work and drink, you'll need to make a new plan to occupy yourself. Going home and staring at a wall will eventually lead to staring at a wall with a drink in your hand.

Don't try to do this alone. Sharing your goals for sobriety with a friend makes all the difference. They can hold you accountable when you're making questionable decisions ("I'm just going to the bar to hang out, I won't drink!") and they can offer a kind ear when you're struggling.

Remind yourself that cravings will pass. Have you ever had that experience when you're sick where you can't remember what it feels like to *not* be sick? The same thing happens with cravings. Give it time, and believe it or not, the feeling will go away.

You'll have to make sacrifices beyond giving up the drug. If you previously used during specific activities (for example: watching a game on TV, going to concerts, or spending time with friends), you may need to make changes. This might mean *not* watching the game, or making new friends who are sober. This can be really hard, but that's what makes it a sacrifice.

Have a plan for when things get bad, because at some point, they will. People get fired, hearts get broken, and sometimes people leave us forever. Develop a plan to get through these major life challenges--without the use of drugs--before they happen.

Don't become complacent with your sobriety. If you someday consider having "just a glass of wine with dinner", don't make the decision lightly. If you've struggled with addiction in the past, you are much more likely to develop an addiction again.

If you do relapse, don't give up. A lot of people find it helpful to keep track of how long they've been sober, but don't confuse this count with the true goal of leading a good life. If you're at day 100 of sobriety, that's great. However, if you make a mistake and end up back at day 0, know that you are not starting over (you gained knowledge, experience, and confidence). In other words: Slipping up is not a license to go on a binge.

Come up with new rituals. How do you celebrate holidays, promotions, or any other happy occasion? If your answer includes any sort of drug, you'll want to get creative and figure out something new. Go wild with a hobby for the day, treat yourself to a nice dinner, or take a weekend trip. Make sure it's something you can get excited about.

My Safety Crisis Plan

Recognize your warning signs and use your coping skills to keep yourself safe and healthy.

Triggers and Stressors

(Behaviors, situations and circumstances that put you at emotional risk)

_____
_____
_____
_____
_____

Things to do...

My goals for healthy behavior:

1. _____
2. _____
3. _____
4. _____
5. _____

People to call...

- 911
- Valley Hospital 602-952-3900
- 1-800-SUICIDE (784-2433)
-
-
-

Warning Signs

(Your behavior signals that show you're growing more and more at risk)

→ Call someone and ask for help.

_____ reports he/she does not have access to prescription medications for use other than as prescribed or access to weapons, lethal medications and/or other means of self-harm.

My Coping Skills...

What I can do to be calm and stay safe IN THE MOMENT:

What can my support person do to help me?

Reminders

➢ Take medications as ordered – do not change the dose or time unless directed by your physician.

➢ If you experience side effects from your medications – notify your outpatient provider or PCP

➢ Keep all aftercare appointments as scheduled – take your copy of aftercare plan to your appointment

tient: _____ Date: _____

When I am Tempted to Use

Check of the situation in which you would most tempted to use drugs or alcohol. Write in your own situations if you do not see them listed.

___ When I am having withdrawals
___ When I want to have just one drink
___ When I want to see if I can handle using in moderation
___ When I have a headache
___ When I am worrying about something
___ When I have a dream about drugs
___ When I am tired
___ When I am in pain
___ When I am depressed
___ When I am angry
___ When I am to relax
___ When I am not a party
___ When I see drugs and alcohol in TV
___ When I am happy
___ When friends are using
___ When I am on vacation

Write your own: _____

SAFETY PLAN

I will cope, calm & soothe myself by:

I will tell myself:

I will call: ☎

I will go to: →

What did you get out of the book overall?

_____
_____
_____
_____
_____
_____
_____
_____
_____
_____
_____
_____

What did you think of this program?

Stepping on the Stones, A New Experience in Recovery

Inventory Sample

Topic: Music

	Family	Relationships	Finance	Addiction	Other	Other
0-10	Nursery rhymes Songs from grandpa	Daycare School	n/a	n/a	Education School songs National anthem	n/a
11-17	Records Tape Sing-a-long	1st song with boyfriend 1st song on date	Buying Tapes and CDs for first time	Music to get high Concerts	Cheers School sings favorites	n/a
18-25	Songs at Wedding	Songs with significant other or children	Buying music	Associated with alcohol and/or drugs use	Favorite music	n/a
26-35	Sing-a-long with children Nursery rhymes	Songs with significant other or children	Buying music	Associated with alcohol and/or drugs use	Favorite music	n/a
36-45	Sing-a-long with children Nursery rhymes	Songs with significant other or children	Buying music	Associated with alcohol and/or drugs use	Favorite music	n/a
46 +	Sing-a-long with grand-children Nursery rhymes	Songs with significant other or grand-children	Buying music	Associated with alcohol and/or drugs use	Favorite music	n/a

Inventory

Topic: _____

	Family	Relationships	Finance	Addiction	Other	Other
0-10						
11-17						
18-25						
26-35						
36-45						
46 +						

Inventory

Topic: _____

	Family	Relationships	Finance	Addiction	Other	Other
0-10						
11-17						
18-25						
26-35						
36-45						
46 +						

Inventory

Topic: _____

	Family	Relationships	Finance	Addiction	Other	Other
0-10						
11-17						
18-25						
26-35						
36-45						
46 +						

Inventory

Topic: _____

	Family	Relationships	Finance	Addiction	Other	Other
0-10						
11-17						
18-25						
26-35						
36-45						
46 +						

Inventory

Topic: _____

	Family	Relationships	Finance	Addiction	Other	Other
0-10						
11-17						
18-25						
26-35						
36-45						
46 +						

Inventory

Topic: _____

	Family	Relationships	Finance	Addiction	Other	Other
0-10						
11-17						
18-25						
26-35						
36-45						
46 +						

Inventory

Topic: _____

	Family	Relationships	Finance	Addiction	Other	Other
0-10						
11-17						
18-25						
26-35						
36-45						
46 +						

Made in the USA
Middletown, DE
18 March 2025

72930356R00155